The Talent Fix

The Talent Fix
Volume 2

A Leader's Guide to Recruiting Great Talent

Tim Sackett

Foreword by Kris Dunn

Society for Human Resource Management
Alexandria, Virginia
shrm.org

Strategic Human Resource Management India
Mumbai, India
shrm.org/in

Society for Human Resource Management
Middle East & North Africa Office
Dubai, UAE
shrm.org/mena

BETTER WORKPLACES
BETTER WORLD™

This publication is designed to provide accurate and authoritative information regarding the subject matter covered. It is sold with the understanding that neither the publisher nor the author is engaged in rendering legal or other professional service. If legal advice or other expert assistance is required, the services of a competent, licensed professional should be sought. The federal and state laws discussed in this book are subject to frequent revision and interpretation by amendments or judicial revisions that may significantly affect employer or employee rights and obligations. Readers are encouraged to seek legal counsel regarding specific policies and practices in their organizations.

This book is published by SHRM. The interpretations, conclusions, and recommendations in this book are those of the author and do not necessarily represent those of the publisher.

SHRM creates better workplaces where employers and employees thrive together. As the voice of all things work, workers, and the workplace, SHRM is the foremost expert, convener, and thought leader on issues impacting today's evolving workplaces. With nearly 325,000 members in 165 countries, SHRM impacts the lives of more than 235 million workers and families globally. Learn more at SHRM.org.

Library of Congress Cataloging-in-Publication Data has been applied for and is on file with the Library of Congress.

ISBN 978-1-586-44638-3 (pbk)
ISBN 978-1-586-44643-7 (pdf)
ISBN 978-1-586-44648-2 (epub)
ISBN 978-1-586-44653-6 (kindle edition)

Printed in the United States of America

PB Printing 10 9 8 7 6 5 4 3 2 1

Contents

Foreword

Sometimes big events happen that you know you'll remember forever. Whether it's the Berlin Wall falling, everyone getting sent home at the start of the lockdown COVID-19 era, or you paying four thousand dollars for two upper deck seats on the Taylor Swift tour, you remember where you were and how you felt.

The Talent Fix going to "Volume Two" is one of those moments.

Okay, that's a tad aggressive. But here we are, and I've been asked to write a new foreword for *The Talent Fix* for my friend and colleague, Tim Sackett. In my previous foreword (Volume One) I focused on Tim, waxing about his ability to demo mediocre recruiting technology (so you don't have to), the current state of his home MSA Detroit (the fast casual scene is buzzing), and the fact he loves to hug people (he even has rules for this).

Let's make this one more about you.

Some of you are browsing the Amazon sample of this book right now, wondering whether this book will help you survive the buzz saw you just walked into. Let's dig into that, because as they say, "I'm from corporate and I'm here to help."

Tim wrote *The Talent Fix* for four distinct types of readers. If you're one of these, odds are you'll get more ROI from *The Talent Fix* than Walter White (*Breaking Bad*) did from his master's degree in chemistry.

YOU'RE A NEW LEADER AND THE RECRUITING FUNCTION IS A "FIXER-UPPER"

This is the leader who rolls in on a given day, and suddenly figures out the recruiting function is not optimized. That's buzzword bingo speak for the more descriptive and informal phrases, "in the toilet," and, "dumpster fire." You're looking at this book right now because you own the recruiting function in some way, and you don't know where to start. Whether you're a C-level, an HR Leader who's never had to recruit, or a rotational high potential recruiter (HiPo) who got plugged into talent acquisition and just wants to do this gig and rotate to marketing in eighteen months, Tim's got your back.

What you'll get in *The Talent Fix* is what you need as a leader. It's a mix of the strategy and tactics you'll need to turn that shack of a recruiting function into a domicile that others will love. Tim's the recruiting industry's version of *Property Brothers* (turning recruiting shops around for sport), except there's only one of him and if he had an industry twin it would be me. Sadly, I'm like a foot taller than him and we can't collectively pull off the looks of Drew and Jonathan Scott, so no TV deal. You'll have to settle for Tim's book.

YOU'RE A RECRUITER WHO WANTS TO DOMINATE

I see you. You're an individual contributor recruiter who's looking for career progression, hates average, and wonders why you aren't running things yet.

STAY THIRSTY, SUPERSTAR

What you're probably missing is the gameplan to run things. Look, I get it—you are awesome at what you do as a recruiter, but what's your plan if you get a chance to run the show in the future? You won't get the job unless you can show that you have a plan, understand how the pieces fit together, and can make the average people on your team better. Steal the ideas in this book and claim them as your own.

If you're looking to hang with someone who will make you better and give you ideas to climb the career ladder at three times the normal speed, you came to the right place. This book is your recruiting MBA. Think of Tim as your recruiting version of Yoda, if Yoda drove a huge Toyota Tundra, owned his own recruiting company, wore an outlier amount of green (Michigan State fan/booster), and mocked me on hikes for not wanting to come within two feet of potential death via five-hundred-foot cliff drops.

YOU'RE A NEWBIE TO THE RECRUITING GAME

Some of you are brand new to the recruiting industry, most likely in your first production recruiting role. You've had success in life, but you've felt how hard and unforgiving this recruiting life can be—most likely when you made your first candidate cold call and couldn't speak because you were sure the candidate would know you were an imposter/fraud. You hung up when the candidate answered your first outbound call, didn't you?

The best way to get comfortable in the recruiting industry is to get your own squad you can look up to. We're all the sum of the five people we spend the most time with. Think of this book as part of your squad, allowing you to level up quicker than you could on your own. Buying this book doesn't mean you can call Tim, but if you close your eyes when he's doing one of the 638 webinars he does every year, it's almost like he's talking to you. Even if he's not.

YOU NEED A CURATOR FOR EMERGING "WORKLEISURE" STYLES

I'd be remiss if I didn't mention that Tim's interested in and can add value to things other than recruiting. For many of the Renaissance people in our lives, that might mean a subspecialty/interest in things like history, stoicism, or oceanography.

Tim can't help you in those areas, but he has great utility in an emerging area—workleisure style. No one slices and dices more Instagram ads on polos and quarter zips than him. Few are marketed to harder by makers of work joggers and dress sneakers than Mr. Sackett. You might not have the access to him like I do as his friend, but if you hit him with a message on LinkedIn in this area, you'll see the value—and end up spending $300 on a Peter Millar hoodie.

I TRUST TIM SACKETT, WHICH MEANS YOU PROBABLY SHOULD ,TOO

I've had some fun with Tim in this foreword, but let's bring the lights down a little bit and cue the soft piano to create a serious mood. I've known Tim Sackett for a decade—and I trust Tim Sackett. Tim's one of the best TA leaders I know, and what I appreciate most about Tim is his no-nonsense approach to the recruiting game.

Tim Sackett has something for each of you. Tim's your guy. Tim's currently doing the work.

Read the book, trust the process, and when you see him live someday in the future—prepare for a full-on hug.[1]

—Kris Dunn, SVP of
Global Talent Acquisition
at Marriott and author of
The Best Boss Ever

Introduction to Volume 2

Usually, this book would have been a "2nd edition." The first edition of *The Talent Fix* was published in 2018. The publisher was like, "Hey, this book is doing pretty good. We should update it and do a second edition. And we also need a new 'red' book!" Seemed super legitimate. I mean, who doesn't need a "red" book on the shelf? It turns out that when you fill a bookstore with books, there aren't many "red" ones, especially in HR.

I hate convention. I also knew I wanted to add a bunch of new stuff, not just update some chapters. A lot has changed since 2018. I also love the movie trilogy *Guardian's of the Galaxy*, which titled each of their movies as volumes: Vol. 1, Vol. 2, and Vol. 3. My vision of updating *The Talent Fix* fit into the volume category! So, *The Talent Fix*, Vol. 2, was created.

The biggest thing you will probably notice in Vol. 2 is that it was mostly written by ChatGPT. Just kidding, AI will never be able to do what a human can do! I pray to myself silently so the AI won't hear me each night. Honestly, the core of the original book is basically the same. I went through each page and thought to myself, "Man, this dude really knows what he's talking about!" I also get invited to book club readings with HR and talent acquisition teams frequently, and the feedback was always stuff like, "This book seems like it was written this year, just for our company!"

The concepts of great talent acquisition haven't really changed over time. It's not some secret sauce that we just made up. Great talent acquisition is and will always be about great talented recruiters, a process that puts candidates first and is easy to navigate, and utilizing the most advanced and proven technology on the market. People. Process. Technology. Execution. Execution is the one thing that is always missed. You can have the best recruiters, the best process, and the best technology and still suck at recruiting. You need to execute all three of those things consistently to be great. Ironically, that's not just in HR or TA. That is the secret sauce to be great in any function.

The features of how we get great in talent acquisition have definitely evolved since the original book. We've gone from machine learning, a subset of artificial intelligence (AI), to full-blown generative AI and conversational AI that will be major game changers in talent acquisition for the foreseeable future. Diversity, equity, inclusion, and belonging (DEIB) continues to evolve as organizations begin to truly reap the advantages of having an inclusive workforce. Marketing technology and advertising continues to push talent acquisition technology makers to rethink how we attract talent to our organizations. On top of all the bright and shiny things to help us get better, we are also getting better at understanding and listening to the psychology of what candidates and employees want out of their job hunting and career experiences.

In Vol. 2, I address a number of things that I left out of the first book and tackle some subjects that we just don't seem to be solving in our industry. I also wanted to try out a few writing concepts that I've been toying around with that I hope you enjoy. Like the original, I'll attempt to do this with a bit of snark, some stories, and concepts that will push you and your team out of their comfort zone.

Recruiting Talent Is Always Hardest in Your Industry?

I started my talent acquisition career when I was 10 years old. My mom started her technical recruiting agency, HRU Technical Resources, in 1980, and she would work at night on her bed calling candidates. She was a single mother, so my sister and I would sit on her bed watching TV with the sound low and listen to her talk to candidates.

These were pre-automated tracking system (ATS) days for a small technical recruiting firm, so she would have to mail a skills checklist to each candidate and then have an administrator at the office key in every skill into a green-screen database. I got ten cents for each skills checklist I folded and stuffed into an envelope. It was a great first recruiting gig for a 10-year-old!

I tell people I was born into recruiting. It's been in my blood since I was a kid. When you sit and listen to your mother question candidates on the phone, you can't help but pick up some tips and tricks along the way. Being a kid of a recruiter may be the best recruiter training of all time.

So, right about now you're thinking, "Great, we get to read Tim's life story."

Not quite—I'll skip ages 0 to 9 and my college years, and other than that, I've been recruiting or in human resources my entire life. So, yeah, throughout this book, you may learn a few things about me. But my hope is you'll learn a lot more about how I believe talent acquisition should run within an organization.

Right out of college mom gave me a job in her company. Lucky for me, I got a raise from the ten-cent envelope stuffing and started out in the recruitment agency environment in a new role she had just learned was the up-and-coming thing in recruiting, a "research assistant."

The research assistant role was basically the precursor to today's sourcing professionals. I worked directly for the recruiters in her company tracking down candidates who were interested in the jobs I had open, and then I would pass them along to the real recruiter to fill in the rest.

In that first job, I learned one of the biggest lies in talent acquisition:

> ### *No one knows how to recruit talent in your industry unless they've worked in your industry!*

This is one giant load of BS!

The only other lie in talent acquisition that comes close to that level is the one about having to work in the job to truly be able to recruit talent in that field. This is the "you need to be a developer to be able to recruit a developer" farce.

I worked for years at Applebee's, a worldwide casual dining chain that serves beer and burgers. It's not that awfully complex, but you can imagine with over two thousand restaurants, there are some challenges.

I left Applebee's to go run talent acquisition at a ten thousand-person hospital system. I still remember sitting in front of the CEO and hearing him say, "You've never worked in healthcare, you have no idea how to recruit a nurse." He was a true believer of the lie above. If I didn't know the industry, how could I ever recruit people to his organization?

So, in this first chapter, I'm going to give you the biggest lie in talent acquisition and the biggest secret! The biggest secret in talent acquisition is:

> ### *Recruiting in every industry is exactly the same!*

It didn't matter to me if I was recruiting a bartender or a critical care registered nurse, the process of making this happen was exactly the same. Also, the bartender and the nurse couldn't care less if I had ever made a drink or delivered critical care to a patient. Those were *their* jobs. My job was to connect them with the people they would be working for who actually knew those jobs.

I've worked in retail, dining, healthcare, and technical, and every single industry is exactly the same. There are challenges. There are buzzwords. There are bad hiring managers. There are good hiring managers. And if I could find talent that was interested in our organization and the positions we had open, then that was all that truly mattered.

The question then is, why do we perpetuate this lie that you must have industry experience to be able to recruit talent for that industry? It's really just basic psychology. If people think your job is super hard then you tend to have more respect and more job security.

If executives thought a monkey could recruit, we would be peeling bananas and fetching them coffee. So, it's to our benefit to get everyone to believe that industry knowledge is super important to uncovering great talent.

So, this may be a good spot, early on, to point out a fact about this book. This is a leader's guide to talent acquisition. I'm writing this book to help leaders better understand talent acquisition, and better help talent acquisition leaders run a more dynamic recruiting shop. Some of this may sting a bit for people not in those roles. It's our job to rise above that so we can understand how and why we've gotten to this point.

Recruiting Isn't Hard

Recruiting isn't difficult. In fact, it's never been easier in the history of the world to find talent. Approximately nine in ten Americans have access to the internet and use it on a daily basis.[1] Everyone who uses the internet is leaving digital exhaust and footprints. Sourcing technology has gotten so advanced that it's basically killing the sourcing function that was just created a decade ago!

You can now find and find out about the majority of candidates you may want to hire. Job boards have collected hundreds of millions of résumés and profiles. On top of that, we all leave a social trail on sites like Facebook, Instagram, X (formerly known as Twitter), Snapchat, and so on.

Within minutes of training a new recruiter who has never recruited a day in his life, we can give them access to millions of potential candidates and have them start contacting them. Of course, these new recruiters will probably be terrible at convincing a candidate to work for your organization, but even a blind squirrel can find a nut occasionally.

I tend to believe we overcomplicate a very simple function. Recruiting is simply about connecting with people who have the desire to work for your organization and the ability to learn the skills needed to work in the positions you need to hire for, if they don't already have them.

The problem so many recruiters face is looking at talent acquisition through our own lens of the organization. If you work inside an organization for any length of time you know what's great about working there, and you know what's awful about working there. Talent acquisition professionals tend to focus way too much on why people wouldn't want to work for their company, rather than why they would want to work there.

I'll talk about this further in Chapter 5 when we look at how to build a great recruiting team, but you can already see that one aspect of being great a talent acquisition is ensuring you have a recruiting team that's all in on the positives of your organization, not the negatives.

Finding pools of talent has never been easier, and that's one main reason recruiting has become more difficult. If you have a pool of ten candidates, that's a pretty easy pool to analyze, screen, and make decisions on who you should hire. If you need to do that with a pool of ten thousand, well, that's not an easy task. But don't allow your team to tell you there's no talent! There's always talent; it just may be out of your league.

When I meet with recruiting teams to try and help them, I constantly hear all the reasons why they can't hire in their organizations. The real reasons? Location, can't pay enough, negative brand, bad leadership, and so forth. The list is endless.

Remember the movie *Indecent Proposal* with Demi Moore and Woody Harrelson? Rich guy says he'll pay $1 million to a husband and wife (Moore and Harrelson) for one night with the wife. The couple needs money. It doesn't mean anything. It's $1 million!

This is recruiting. The rich guy was testing the market. Candidates all have a price. Some great talent you may be able to get cheap because their personal market cap is less than they could get. Some, you will have to pay an incredible amount to get—so much so, you may not even bother.

To keep everything equitable within our organizations, we tend to want to pay similar talent a similar wage. This engineer is average talent, so we can pay him $100,000; this other engineer is an exceptional talent, so we can pay her $120,000. When another great talent comes around and wants to work for you but wants $140,000, we now believe we have a recruiting problem.

You don't have a recruiting problem. The talent is there; you just aren't willing to pay for the talent you want, so now you have to make concessions. Often, we get so caught in this concessions loop that we become noncompetitive in the recruiting market.

"Well, Joe is our best engineer and he's worked for us for ten years and received normal raises. Engineers on the market with less skill want us to pay them more than Joe. We can't do that." Sound familiar? This is what makes recruiting hard.

Recruiting is not just about finding talent. We already know that finding talent is easy. Finding talent that will accept our average pay and benefits? Now that's hard!

Over the past decade or two it's become extremely popular, especially among the media, to talk about how people don't care about money as the primary factor in accepting or staying at a job. They cite studies indicating that people care more about all the other things, like career development, challenging work, and so forth.

But, when you dig into these studies, you find what researchers have known for a long time: Money matters until it doesn't. Think about that for a second. Of course, we all want to work for a company with great leaders and in a position that will challenge us and develop us.

But if we can't pay our bills, none of that matters. It doesn't matter that you have ping pong tables and hot yoga on Wednesday nights if your employees can't figure out how to pay the rent. The idea that "money matters until it doesn't" means that you have to be willing to pay at the market minimum if you truly want to be in the recruiting game.

You probably have to pay more than market if you suck at some things—for example, if you have bad managers or a bad brand image.

Therein lies the vicious cycle of why organizations fail. Can't get great talent, projects fail, revenue drops, and we can't pay higher wages, so now we have to pay lower than the market, which means we get worse talent. The cycle continues.

Did I say recruiting was easy?! Ugh, recruiting is hard!

You Are Not a Unicorn

I hate going to recruiting conferences and listening to anyone who works at Google or used to work at Google. Why? Google is a unicorn. They have unlimited funds for talent acquisition, the best technology on the planet, and the best employment brand on the planet. They lead the market in pay and benefits. Thus, they can hire just about anyone they want.

You and I are not unicorns.

Most of us are plow horses at best, some of us may be racehorses, and there are probably a few donkeys among us as well. When you compare yourself to a unicorn, you're always going to seem ugly. Unicorns are magical and beautiful and mythical.

The great thing about talent acquisition is that comparing ourselves to unicorns in every industry is basically worthless, and when you dig in deep enough you find that many of those unicorns telling us how to fix all of our problems aren't really that much better than we are.

Laszlo Bock, Google's head of HR, in his book *Work Rules!* famously came out and said that his own talent acquisition process, on which the company spent hundreds of millions of dollars to make perfect, was only 1 percent better than a 50/50 coin flip.[2] Google would have been farther ahead just to bring in candidates from day one, flip a coin, and use that selection method to pick talent.

Imagine all the money and time it would have saved! I'll give Google credit for sharing this information because most don't. In 2014, online shoe retailer Zappos announced it was going to do away with job postings. We are so famous and so awesome we don't even have to post jobs. We'll just pluck the candidates we want out of thin air. That lasted all of about zero days. The company's IT team never got on board because it turns out people want to know what jobs you have open, and if you don't let them know, they don't show much interest in coming to work for you.

The unicorn theory of talent acquisition ruins more leaders in our industry than any other single factor. You come in day one and tell the CEO, "We're going to be just like Facebook," and eighteen months later, you get fired because you haven't even reached MySpace, let alone Facebook.

So, should we never strive to be the best? No, you should. But some organizations are beyond being the best; they've reached a status unreachable by a "normal" organization. To reach unicorn status, you have to have this crazy combination of insane, sustained success, once-in-a-lifetime leaders, and a desired consumer brand. Basically, you have to be transcendent.

We should strive to be great, but we need to define what great is, and great is not Google. Google is beyond great. Great for your organization may be to have the most recognized employment brand within your city, region, or within your industry. Maybe it's being the employer of choice within a certain segment of talent in your industry or marketplace. Great may be leading your industry in retention or productivity. The key is to define what greatness is for you, not what it is in comparison to some other organization that isn't you.

As a talent acquisition leader, that's the first conversation I'm having with my CEO. Not day one on the job. I'm having that conversation with the CEO during my interview. I don't want to accept a job that is doomed to fail over unreachable expectations. If my CEO wants to be like Google, then they should go hire Laszlo, but I'll bet even Laszlo won't accept that job because he knows how rare unicorns are!

That first conversation with a CEO lets me know if we can ever be truly great at talent acquisition. It takes an all-in commitment from the senior leadership team and a visionary CEO to make this happen, to be great. It doesn't mean you can't be really really good at talent acquisition with a schmuck of a CEO. You can, but not great!

I'm looking for a CEO who owns the talent in the organization. In fact, there's one question I implore you to ask your own leadership team:

Who owns talent in our organization?

If they don't say "I do" or "We do," you're in trouble. If they say, "Well, that's why we are hiring you. You own talent," run, don't walk. Run out of that organization. Talent acquisition doesn't own talent in any organization. Leaders need to own the talent on their teams. Talent acquisition is the tool that helps them attract the best talent, improve their talent, and uncover talent.

Talent acquisition doesn't own talent, not at least until they allow me to make the final hiring decision on every hire that comes into my barn. If that's the case, I get a final say on who is hired and who is not hired, then I'll say I own talent as a talent acquisition leader. I have yet to meet one CEO or leader who was willing to give that much power to recruiting.

The Noise Is Deafening to Candidates

As more organizations ramp up their recruitment marketing and candidate experience programs, the noise surrounding candidates is at an all-time high and getting worse. What do I mean when I say "noise"?

Noise is everything a candidate potentially has to sift through when determining if a job and a company are right for them. The noise then is all of the stuff you create and send out, which is pretty traditional, but now includes online sources, like review sites (Glassdoor, Indeed, Reddit), social media sites (Facebook, LinkedIn, X [formerly known as Twitter]), bloggers, local meetup groups, and more, that just create a seemingly unending source of additional noise.

The noise has gotten so bad that most candidates don't tune it out, but they begin to believe that it's all the same. That one crappy Glassdoor review then becomes weighed on the same level as your career site video of an employee speaking about how great it is to work for your company. Ultimately, they end up washing each other out in terms of importance, which leaves the candidate trying to decide on their own what to believe.

Welcome to the life of a marketer. Marketing spends all their time attempting to get people to have a positive, trusting view of the product or service they're supporting. Now, talent acquisition is being put in the same boat, attempting to get candidates to trust in the content that we are creating, but not listen to all the other content that is organically being created by the community around us.

> *One of the keys to being great at talent acquisition isn't necessarily being a great company to work for; it's managing the noise better than everyone else that's in the same market for the talent your organization needs.*

Of course, you want to be a great organization to work for, but most organizations aren't great, they're just average. This is a place that's pretty good most of the time, great sometimes, awful very rarely, so when it's all said and done, your employees will say, "Yeah, I like where I work." The top 10 percent may even "love" working for you, and our hope is almost no one will hate it.

If you can control the noise in your market better than others, you have a better shot at getting the talent you want. This means you need to do employee branding and recruitment marketing better than anyone else. The noise you create doesn't need to be louder than the outside forces in your market, but your noise better be heard by those in the market who need to hear it.

How do you do this? First, it has to be real and compelling. Assuming you provide competitive benefits and pay, a 401(k) match, paid time off, and so on, you need a marketing strategy to differentiate your noise from others'. What differentiates your noise is transparency. It's your leaders, hiring managers, and employees speaking the truth, from the heart.

Getting to this point for many is really hard to do because we've been conditioned by legal and HR for decades to keep everything super buttoned up. One great thing in the past decade that's come out of Silicon Valley and many of the young entrepreneurs who run companies in the technology industry is their natural ability to be "real" with their employees, customers, and stakeholders.

The transparency they show is a strong departure from the corporate America we are used to hearing from. These young leaders speak with passion and a bit of naivety, but their noise reaches their targets like an arrow.

Remember in the classic *Peanuts* specials when the teacher spoke, it was just rambling mumbles that were incoherent? This is what most candidates and even our employees are hearing right now when traditional leaders speak: "Wah wah wah wah." For those leaders who are speaking with transparency, it's like the joy Odysseus experienced listening to the sirens in *The Odyssey*! Okay, both of those references are a bit dated if you're under 30! Go Google them!

So, one clear way of breaking through the noise to candidates is transparency of message. Not the washed, vanilla message we've been creating in talent acquisition for decades, but one that actually tells candidates what it's like to be a part of your organization, and is told by your employees in their own, unscripted words.

Another way to get your transparent message across is to get others who aren't a part of your normal tribe to speak your truth. Alumni employees, partner organizations, community leaders you're working on projects with, universities who send their students to you, and so forth. People tend to listen to parties who don't have any vested interest in your success or failure with a more trusting ear.

Chapter 10 will dig into this concept in detail. Recruitment marketing and employment branding are all the rage in talent acquisition, but when we boil it down, it all comes back to this transparency of message and getting candidates to trust your brand, your team, and the notion that their career will be better by working for your organization.

Recruiting One Candidate Is the Same in Every Organization, But . . .

If you only had to recruit one candidate, the process is virtually the same at every single organization on the planet. But enterprise-level talent acquisition is a completely different animal than talent acquisition for small and medium-sized businesses (SMBs) and even most large-sized organizations.

When you hire one candidate, the process becomes pretty simple. You understand your need. You determine how you'll fill that need. You execute the sourcing. You screen. You interview. You hire. Once that one need becomes thousands of needs, the process no longer stays simple. It's not just about scaling a process.

Hiring one hundred candidates per year is completely different from hiring one hundred thousand candidates. The complexity of hiring tens of thousands of employees per year is a completely different beast. You don't go from running talent acquisition for an organization that hires one hundred people to running a talent acquisition department hiring ten thousand people overnight.

I'm fascinated by enterprise talent acquisition as well. Branding, compliance, technology, marketing, and so on, all get ramped up at a level most SMB talent acquisition leaders can't even fathom. By the same token, the number of hats one SMB talent acquisition leader has to wear on a daily basis would overwhelm the most seasoned enterprise talent acquisition leader.

This book is primarily designed to help non-enterprise-level talent acquisition leaders.

Conceptually, you can take most of the ideas presented within this book and scale them, but hiring at enterprise is like running an entire other business. This isn't to say that hiring at the enterprise level is harder (although it may be for some organizations); it's just different from hiring in organizations that may only hire one thousand employees or fewer annually, which covers most businesses worldwide.

This is a guide for those who have experience and want to get better at and improve talent acquisition at their organization; for those talent acquisition professionals moving into leadership roles; talent acquisition leaders of one, two, or five employees; talent acquisition leaders who not only run their departments, but also have their own requisitions to fill.

You guys are my tribe. The entire reason I started blogging nine years ago was I thought I had some ideas, tips, and tricks that could help other talent acquisition leaders who were struggling. Almost daily, I receive a message from another talent acquisition leader like myself asking for some sort of help. Often, the question they're asking is simply, "What would you do if you were me, in my current circumstance? How would you run talent acquisition at this organization, and what steps would you take to make it better?"

So, now you know what the rest of this book is about. It's the answer to that one question: If I were you, and I was asked to run talent acquisition at your organization, what would I do? I think some of these suggestions will challenge you to think about your own talent acquisition department and how it's currently being run. My hope is you'll try and test out certain pieces you think you can implement, save some for later, and throw out the stuff that doesn't make sense for your specific situation.

That's what great talent acquisition leaders will do. They will tackle the low-hanging fruit first, focus on the biggest impact they can make in the least amount of time for the fewest resources, then move systematically on to bigger and harder systemic problems that need to be fixed. Get some easy wins. Get your legs under you. Get your team acting and thinking positively. Get your executives to have confidence in you and your team.

It all starts with hiring one candidate. Everyone can do that!

Here's the thing . . .

Recruiting is recruiting. Your jobs aren't unique butterflies that are harder to fill than some other jobs in an industry or organization that is also trying to hire. If you are amazing at recruiting, you can recruit anywhere at any time. And you definitely don't need to know how to do the job you're recruiting for to be good at recruiting candidates for that job. We all just like to believe that our recruiting job is the hardest recruiting job. All recruiting jobs are hard.

» 2 «

Talent Acquisition Is the New HR

It feels pretty good to be in talent acquisition right now. Remember when talent acquisition was just one of those silos under human resources? Talent acquisition used to be treated like Cinderella before she became a princess! Payroll, benefits, employee relations, and all the other "step-sisters" would tell us we didn't have any skills or value and then talk about their SHRM certifications and laugh behind our backs.

Then this crazy thing happened. It's really hard to pinpoint the first time this phrase was ever used by a CEO, but we can safely say it was probably a couple of decades ago when some well-meaning CEO made this statement, most likely at a shareholder meeting or earnings call:

Our employees are our most valuable asset.

This was the first sign that talent acquisition was going to have a bigger role in organizations of the future. At first, this was all about taking care of, developing, and retaining our current workforce. That was, and mostly still is, the job of human resources, although I'll lay out an argument in this chapter on how this is beginning to change.

Let's move forward a bit from almost every single leader on the planet believing employees were valuable assets to when not having enough employees started to become a potential business hazard to growth and profit! That was the tipping point. Because your employees are your most valuable asset, and businesses are in business to collect assets, being able to acquire more assets then becomes a super valuable skill to have in an organization.

Say hello to my little friend, the forgotten talent acquisition department!

I will argue that the talent acquisition department in a modern organization may be the single most valuable differentiator an organization can have, next to a killer sales and marketing department. We can argue chicken or the egg, but if you can hire the best talent in your market, and you can sell the heck out of your products and services, you're going to win many more times than you'll lose.

I know some people will argue that technology is more important (innovation, creativity, and so on), but I consistently demo talent acquisition technology products that are incredible, but can't stay in business for more than a year because they make bad hires and can't sell.

What's nice about being the new prettiest girl on the block, as talent acquisition currently is, is that you get lots of attention. It's both a gift and a curse. If you're a really good talent acquisition leader, you love the attention. If you suck, you hate the attention. Because of the importance that talent acquisition has in every organization now, I see more talent acquisition leaders getting fired than ever before.

Being valuable and important comes with some pressure to perform. Talent acquisition used to be able to hide behind HR and leaders would just think HR sucked. *Fast Company* famously published the article "Why We Hate HR" in 2005, which may have been the official launch of talent acquisition trying to separate itself from our big sister's apron strings.

If your leaders believe HR sucks and doesn't add value, then it doesn't help you as a talent acquisition leader to stay on that sinking ship, which to be honest, has been bailing water since the Great Recession. On the flip side, talent acquisition has been continuing to grow and strengthen its hold as many CEOs' favorite department.

All of this leads to right now being the perfect time to be in talent acquisition and the perfect time to have your organization's leaders on your side to build a world class talent acquisition department. Your organization needs talent more than ever. Your CEO and senior executive team don't know how to do this and are waiting for you to tell them the next steps they need to take.

What they need from you is the plan (which is why you're reading this) and then you need to execute that plan. It sounds so easy! We know it's not. But still, it's better to be in this situation than in the situation where your organizational leaders aren't looking at you for help or as the solution to their largest problem of finding talent to grow and sustain your business.

Another key to great talent acquisition leadership is simply this:

Develop a plan.
Have great confidence that your plan will work.
Ask for all the resources you need to execute your plan.
Shut up.

We tend to suck as negotiators when asking for the tools and resources we need to be great. I'll blame our HR DNA in that HR has, for its entire history, thrown itself on the sword when budgeting time came around and offered to "do more with less." You know who doesn't do more with less? Every other department in your company! Sales never says, "Hey, give us less and we'll produce 15 percent more sales than last year!"

We are expert negotiators when it comes to closing candidates, but somehow we crumble during budgeting time when telling the organization what it is we need to execute our plan. Marketing is always the best; we need to follow their lead. Marketing constantly says, "Yeah, well, we'll need a 25 percent budget increase to drive a 10 percent sales increase," then a year later when there was a 3 percent sales decline, says, "Yeah, this year we'll need a 40 percent budget increase to catch up!"

Great talent acquisition leaders will definitely make things happen with whatever tools and resources they are given, but let's not kid ourselves. If obtaining talent is an organizational imperative, putting the resources behind that imperative is also a necessity. Don't allow yourself, as a talent acquisition leader, to agree to deliverables you know you can't get without having the resources to support it. This is how and why most talent acquisition leaders lose their jobs.

Your Organization's Next Big Talent Acquisition Threat

Having a well-oiled talent acquisition machine may be the least of your worries in the coming years. There are so many futurists that claim they know what the future of HR and talent acquisition will be, but the reality is, it's all just educated guesses.

The flavor of choice right now is that robots are the future. Boy, I hope so! Wouldn't that be awesome if you could have a robot do all your work? Our reality is automation and technology have been around for decades in talent acquisition and it won't stop anytime soon.

A much more likely issue we will face is having a serious shortage of real humans in the workforce. Prior to the start of the Great Recession in December 2007, it was widely reported that the US labor market would be hit with mass retirements as the Baby Boomers left the workforce en masse. It was called the "Gray Wave" or the "Silver Tsunami."

The National Institute for Occupational Safety and Health reports that one in four workers was over the age of 55 as of the year 2021.[1] As the Baby Boomers increasingly reach retirement age, the rate at which they'll leave the workforce will increase as well.[2]

At its peak, the Boomer generation reached 78.8 million people, while the millennials number 75.4 million. The Census Bureau projects Generation X to hit its peak in 2018 with a not-so-whopping 13 million people fewer than Boomers' highest (65.8 million). Boomers are retiring at a rate of 10,000 per day, so that's another 3.6 million a year leaving the workforce.[3]

Luckily for all of us in recruiting, we got a stay of execution and were delivered a different sentence by the Great Recession. Instead of not having enough workers, we all of sudden had too many workers. Many of us followed traditional ways of shrinking our workforce through lay-offs, rewarding tenure over performance, and basically keeping our older workforce.

These are decisions organizations and leadership make. In hindsight, I'm sure many would like a second chance at how they handled this situation. What it left was a hole of leadership that will take us more than a decade to fill. Not only did we keep our more tenured workers, but we also stopped developing our workforce of the future, compounding an already looming problem.

Your organizations are facing a worker shortage problem in the near future. It won't hit you all at once. It's not like the time to fill a position will jump suddenly from twenty-three to sixty-three days! It will gradually go up, little by little, until all of sudden you're shocked at what it's become.

Let me give you a list of the most popular ways to handle worker shortages:

- Be the greatest company and brand in your market that everyone wants to be. Places like Google, Facebook, Nike, and so on. (Hard to achieve and rare.)
- Pay more than everyone else in your market. (Expensive.)
- Have a unique benefit or structure that others are unwilling to do. This could be things like remote workforce, ultra-cool modern work environment, unique leadership philosophy, and so on. (Risky.)
- Hire any warm body willing to work for you, and churn and burn constantly. (Stupid.)
- Develop and grow your own workforce. (Expensive short term, but cost effective long term, and takes leadership vision to accomplish.)

That's really about it. You either buy a workforce or you grow a workforce. I guess we didn't talk about what could be an ultimate future prognostication of talent acquisition: What if organizations rewarded their employees for having future workers? Could you imagine?

"Hey Bob, look, we've got a hole in our workforce plan for 2038. Do you think you and your wife could pick us up on this one? We'll pay for everything, including setting aside a college education with little Bobbie's name on it."

I don't think I've read any futurists thinking this may be the future of recruitment, but I wouldn't sleep on this idea—that's how serious I think the problem with our aging workforce is. Before we get to the point of paying for our workers to have babies, I do think we are going to see some serious changes to workforce flexibility and how our workers perform their work.

A 70-year-old worker may not want to work 40 hours a week as an engineer, but they might be willing to give us a couple of days a week. Right now, most US business leaders look down on this concept. This will have to change. I would rather have 16 hours of Mary helping me improve my processes than no Mary at all.

This will bring on an entirely new issue for talent acquisition leaders who are now managing around filling different sized gaps within the workforce, not just full-sized pieces. Some are already a bit better at this; talent acquisition (TA) departments in healthcare and hospitals facing massive nursing shortages are showing us the way.

In nursing, jobs requiring people with special skills need to have coverage over a certain time. When we look at current and worsening labor shortages in the technology and accounting industries, similar views will have to be taken. How do we "cover" a full-time mechanical engineer job with three people? It's fraught with complexity, but someone will figure it out eventually.

Regardless, talent acquisition leaders need to be on the forefront of conversations about how talent is being built at every level of the organization. Most TA leaders today are only having one conversation around how to bring in more new people with the skill sets we need.

As TA leaders, we also need to have the conversations with our leadership about how we are growing our current workers who have proven to be loyal, good performers to fill future roles. This is basic succession, which is traditionally left for HR, and it's mostly been a failure across the board.

When I speak to HR and TA leaders about their technology needs, one system will constantly come up—succession. Everyone thinks they need a technology solution to solve employee succession, but the reality is, technology can do nothing to solve your succession problems. Succession will be solved when your leadership team makes it a priority and lets you "overhire" the bodies you need to start building those plans.

The biggest problem with succession is that we want results and plans, but are unwilling to put resources behind building our workforce of the future. You can't have your current workforce and that capacity, and have your future workforce and that capacity, in the same group of people. The laws of physics won't allow it!

Why am I talking about this in a talent acquisition book? I believe the success of a talent acquisition leader is predicated on making it easier for your team to fill really difficult positions and if you build an internal workforce pipeline through succession, you can look like the most amazing TA leader of all time.

Talent Acquisition Needs to Own Retention

Okay, this leads me one of my critical keys to being great at talent acquisition:

Every employee you can stop from leaving your organization is one fewer position you need to fill in talent acquisition.

See, I told you in Chapter 1 that I'm not the most sophisticated guy on the planet when it comes to talent acquisition operational excellence. For me, talent acquisition is a fairly straightforward, easy process if I have openings and I need to fill openings.

If I don't have openings to fill, my job gets super easy and I look like a rock star!

Another piece of heavy lifting we've left up to our HR brothers and sisters is retention. I want talent acquisition to take retention back, to own it completely. Remember how I told you not to own talent acquisition? Well, now you get to own something! You now own retention of all employees.

Why? Go read the statement above. HR cares about retaining employees, but they really don't have any skin in the game. Talent acquisition truly cares about retention because every time someone decides to leave our organization, or we decide for them, it creates more work for us.

I'm not saying HR doesn't care, but if they fire Timmy on Friday, it probably makes their life easier, while it will definitely make our life harder. Don't read into this that I think talent acquisition should keep bad performers. That is not at all what I'm saying. Everybody in the organization needs to be on board with firing bad people fast.

I don't hire to fire. I hire truly believing that the employee will be a great and productive citizen that will work three decades and get a nice gold watch at their retirement party, or whatever you give out at your retirement parties. I hire hoping and believing this employee will be around for years and years.

Now, we all know that isn't the case for every hire. Sometimes we miss on a few hires or so. Sometimes, someone sneaks through the process who we think will be great, but they suck. The problem is, we tend to hang on to bad hires way too long. Like, way, way, way too long!

We have jokes in HR about organizations where all you need to do is get hired, and you'll have a job for life because they're known for almost never firing bad performers. When I was running HR for a large region at Applebee's, we had biannual management performance calibration meetings. These meetings would last full days and the process was to calibrate all of our management teams by performance across a large area.

What you found fairly quickly in these meetings was that the top performers rise to the top very quickly. We all knew who they were and why they were good. The very bottom performers also were fairly easy to spot. The ones who drove us nuts were the long-term low performers who were just good enough not to be the worst.

We called these chronic low performers the "tallest of the seven dwarfs." They were still bad, but just good enough not to get fired that day. As leaders, it was frustrating that we held on to low performers too long, but it seemed like we never had the pipeline of incoming talent where we could make the call to let them go and risk leaving a team short.

At Applebee's is where I first experienced what we called a "save strategy" when it came to talent and retention. I've since seen and heard of similar plans at other companies that focused on doing whatever it took to keep an employee with the organization.

If we knew who our best performers were and what their value was to us, it made sense that we would do anything to ensure they stayed with our organization. At Applebee's, if we found out a top performer was about to leave or put in their notice, we instantly set off a process to "save" that employee.

If a high-performing general manager (GM) of a restaurant was found to be looking for another job, however it was determined, their boss instantly had to let their next-level supervisor know, as well as the highest HR person in their region.

These three folks would then game plan on next steps. This usually meant the three of us would get in front of that person as soon as possible, in the next twenty-four hours. Time is of the essence when you find out someone is thinking of leaving. Many employees will get so far down the path of leaving, they truly believe they can't turn back.

After meeting with the GM, it would be determined if there was something the three of us could do to save this person, or if it needed to be elevated to the executive level. Most often, the first and second levels of leadership could solve the issue. We would frequently find someone would be leaving over issues that were easily solved. More money, of course, was common, but it was also schedule, location, strained internal relationships, and so on. We were given all the freedom we needed to solve these issues, understanding that the end goal was not to create even worse issues.

If the problem was deemed unsolvable and the GM still wanted to leave our employ, we then elevated it to the corporate headquarters and the save team included the CHRO, CEO, and COO. Pretty big folks to bring into the process. This may have happened a total of ten times per year, but it did happen.

At this point, we would buy the GM an airline ticket and stick them on a plane to Kansas City, MO, the headquarters of Applebee's at the time. We would put them up in a hotel room and arrange transportation. The KC save team would move their schedules around to accommodate the incoming GM and they would have the "talk."

"Tell us, why do you want to leave?" "What will it take to keep you?" This was re-recruitment at the highest level! No egos. No power play. Everything was about, how do we keep an employee who is high performing and wanting to leave us? There must be something we are failing at and we need to fix it. Not a blame game. We truly looked for solutions for someone we want to keep.

The save strategy was effective about 60 percent of the time, which is huge! Also, I never felt like I sat in front of one of the managers who was using the strategy against us. It's a huge risk to come forward and say you're going to leave, all as a play to get something you want. The team may have deemed you weren't worthy. Now, on top of not getting what you want, you're viewed as a liar!

At the restaurant level, hourly workers were treated the same way. Remember, we didn't hire to fire, or to just let you walk out. Our goal was to hire great people, train them well, and help them do their job the best they could. So, if a high-performing hourly worker wanted to leave, the restaurant-level leadership would do a similar save strategy internally.

This would never work in a broken culture. We had a very strong culture at Applebee's that was about doing the right thing by our people and rewarding high performance. The save strategy guaranteed that high performers were a priority. This didn't mean that if an average performer wanted to leave we wouldn't work to save them. We would. Our goal was to make them high performing as well, but we may not go as far to save an average performer.

The save strategy is the best example of retention that I've ever heard from any organization, ever. Lucky for me, I got to witness its power firsthand and see how it helped solidify and drive culture. Also, if it was determined that we couldn't save someone, the support did not end. We had individuals who were awesome restaurant managers who dreamed of being something else. If we could support them on that venture, it usually came back to us in positive ways, through referrals, recommendations, or helping out in a pinch.

At Applebee's, operations, HR, training, and the executive leadership were all held accountable for employee retention. It was tied into our annual bonuses. It's not enough to have it be part of your job, there had to be some skin in the game for all of us if we truly wanted to make an impact.

Remember the HR darling Zappos? It seemed like for most of the decade you couldn't go to an HR or TA conference without someone from Zappos speaking. The online shoe retailer had arguably the most innovative HR and TA shop on the planet with visionary leadership that believed people were truly the key to being a great business.

They believed it so strongly they were willing to put cash behind their hires.[4] After finishing the first ninety days of training, each new employee was offered $1,000 to leave the company. It was the talk of HR when the practice first became public a decade ago. (By the way, Zappos now offers $4,000 after training for employees to leave.)

Then a really crazy thing happened. In an industry where everyone copies everyone, almost no one followed Zappos's policy. Why?

It's a brilliant strategy! It may be the best retention, culture, and engagement idea to come out of HR ever, in history! The cost of turnover is massive, and $1,000 is nothing to pay to get rid of a bad hire or a hire that is disengaged. I would argue it's the best investment your organization could ever make.

Organizations haven't followed suit because deep down in places we don't talk about at parties, we know the truth. We know if we offered new employees cash to leave, many would take it. They would take it for so many reasons. I could write another book on just this topic.

Most of us don't really even know what makes a candidate we hire a good hire for our organization. We don't trust that our managers are really developing and inspiring their teams. We know we hire talent that probably isn't the best fit, but they're "good enough."

Zappos doesn't hire "good enough" talent. In 2009, when Amazon acquired Zappos, most probably thought the practice would stop, but it didn't. Jeff Bezos, the CEO of Amazon, doubled-down on the practice in Amazon's own fulfillment centers and made it better.

Amazon decided not only is it important to catch bad hires early, like Zappos, but also it is important to catch those actively disengaged employees throughout their tenure. Amazon offers $1,000 after training for employees to leave, and then increases that amount each annual review after a year for five years.

That's $5,000 to leave your Amazon job at your five-year anniversary if you truly feel its not a great place to work. So, each year, for five years, managers are having this conversation with their employees. "Are you all in? If not, we totally understand, here's some cash, enjoy the rest of your life."

This is talent acquisition at a level most organizations won't reach, and not because Amazon and Zappos are unicorns. Most organizations won't reach this level for the simple fact we don't have the guts it takes to present this program to our executives and then put the processes, practices, and plans in place to make it happen.

I frequently get asked by TA leaders what is something they can do today to make their recruitment better at their organization. My answer is always, stop losing people. Okay, it's really stop losing the right people.

Posting and Praying Is Dead

There is one primary recruiting strategy that is by far more popular than any other. It's used by 100 percent of organizations and is the primary, single strategy for roughly 90 percent of corporate talent acquisition shops. What is it? Post and pray!

Let me explain because most people reading this right now are saying to themselves, "Well, our team doesn't post and pray!" And the reality is, you're probably lying to yourself, or just don't know any better.

Post and pray means that your talent acquisition team

- Meets with hiring managers and gets job specs;
- Posts the job in your ATS, which then posts it to your career site and other integrated job board type sites (e.g., LinkedIn, CareerBuilder, Indeed, Google for Jobs);
- Accepts all of the applications and résumés that come in from those postings;
- Reaches out to those who applied and does some level of basic screening for your hiring manager;
- Contacts recruitment agencies when your hiring managers start getting antsy; and
- Rinses and repeats for every position you have.

That's 90 percent of corporate talent acquisition, at least in the United States, across all size enterprises. If this is most of your team's activity, you will eventually lose your job in talent acquisition because this is not talent acquisition. This is posting and praying.

The next level beyond post and pray is where your recruiters will go onto a job board site and try to reach out for some candidates who have posted their profile or résumé on the site, but haven't applied to your job. Congratulations if your team does this consistently: you've now reached the top 25 percent of corporate talent acquisition shops.

This is "sourcing lite." Not real sourcing, but at least you're not just sitting around praying someone will apply to your job. Take credit for getting to this point, seriously! You have no idea how many TA shops never will. If you really want to up your game, start having them go back into your ATS database and contact candidates who applied previously. Then you'll fully be running with scissors!

I only joke about this a little. It does not take much to be considered good at talent acquisition because we've set the bar so low for so long. It would be safe to say that 20 percent of corporate TA shops only post their jobs to their own career site and nowhere else. I call this the "lost dog strategy" of recruiting.

The lost dog recruiting strategy is based on how an 8-year-old child would find their lost dog. Have you ever lost a pet? I have; it's an awful feeling. What's the first thing a parent tells a child when a pet runs away from home? First, "Don't worry, we'll find them," and then, "Let's make some posters to put around the neighborhood!"

If you lose your dog, you need to make lost dog posters! It's Lost-Dog-Finding Strategy 101. Take a big box of crayons, construction paper, pictures of Fido, and bam! You've got a strategy already in the works.

An 8-year-old instinctively knows how to find his dog when it runs away. Kids don't sit in their house or on the front porch and wait for Fido to come home. They go out and advertise and search in the area where more than likely they or someone else would have seen the dog.

When you only post your jobs on your career site, you're basically saying an 8-year-old child knows how to find talent better than you. Only posting on your website is like losing your dog and making one poster and placing that poster on the front door of your house.

Your only hope of finding your dog is if someone finds your dog, begins walking around your neighborhood, and happens to spot your house and your poster. Your job posting on your career site is that one poster hanging on your front door.

We tend to overestimate how popular we are with candidates within our marketplace, and become perplexed when we post a position, and great talent doesn't immediately come out of the woodwork and apply. Even talent in the market who want to work for us don't apply because they have no idea you posted the job.

It's really hard when you work every day to better your organization to believe no one is really looking at your career site and visiting your jobs, but for the most part that's true. There are over six million companies in the United States alone.[5]

In your own market, candidates have hundreds, if not thousands, of options to work. Do you truly think they're visiting your career page every day, week, even year? They're not.

We want to believe we work at the best place and everyone wants to come work for us, but our reality is less sexy. Which means you can't rely on your career site to drive great talent to your company. Sure, it's one factor that can help, but if it's your major factor, you're in big trouble. The lost dog recruitment strategy is alive and well, and it's a little sad.

In the coming chapters, I'll explain how you go beyond post and pray, and for sure lost dog strategy. There isn't one perfect approach, but there are foundational approaches to recruiting that can set up every organization for success. Also, for the skill sets it will take to be successful in talent acquisition in the future, posting and praying is not a future-looking skill set for great talent acquisition.

We started this chapter by saying talent acquisition is the new HR. I want to amend that by saying that talent acquisition has grown into its own function as a peer to HR. I don't want to be HR; I want to be better than HR. I don't want to the stereotypical redheaded stepchild of the organization. (By the way, if that offends you, I'm sorry. I'm just giving you an accurate description of myself: redheaded stepchild. What I usually find is no one gets offended at ginger jokes, not even gingers.)

Talent acquisition has the opportunity to be the driving force behind every company, but only if we become dynamic and change the way we go about taking care of our business. Our business is people. We're the real "people business." We find the talent that will help our companies grow and succeed. Without us, the entire organization is just praying for a miracle.

Here's the thing . . .

If you're in talent acquisition, you have great influence in your organization. Every single CEO in the world will say something to the effect of, "talent is our most important asset." That means you work in the most important function in your organization, as identified by your CEO. While that's awesome, you also work in the most visible function in your company. Use that influence to get the tools and resources you need to be successful. Don't allow your function to be undervalued.

Every TA Problem Can Be Solved by Money

That's it. That's the chapter!

We love to believe this isn't true. We will tell ourselves that it's not all about money and people don't leave companies; they leave managers and other really bad advice we've read in the media for the last few decades.

The truth is that people will work the worst job in the world for a very long time if they are overpaid. They'll work for the most awful boss for a very long time if they are overpaid. They'll work for the worst company if they are overpaid. They put up with the worst commute imaginable if they are overpaid.

Need more applicants? I can get you more with enough money. Need your new hires to stay on longer? I can get them to stay longer with great retention bonuses. Need more referrals? Okay, money doesn't really impact referrals! But you get the picture.

The reason we wanted to believe money couldn't solve our problems in talent acquisition (TA) is because we didn't control the money. If you don't control it, you better focus on something you can control or at least find some other stuff to blame for your failures.

If you give me enough money, I can solve any TA problem you have—every single one.

This issue is that we don't have unlimited money, which is why we have to fix all the other stuff. If all compensation were the same from company to company, then money wouldn't matter. Also, small amounts of money matter. You might not leave your job for another dollar more per hour, but many, many people will. Don't place your levels of acceptance onto others.

Everyone has a number in their head that allows them to put up with something they don't want to. What's your number? How much did someone pay you to give up on your dreams? I bet it was far less than you ever imagined.

Money matters. It's always mattered. Stop acting like it doesn't.

Here's the thing . . .

Every TA problem can be solved by money.

» 4 «

Building Your "Perfect" Talent Acquisition Department

Okay, I get it. There's no such thing as perfect, but I love the aspirational aspect that just maybe there's a "perfect" talent acquisition (TA) design and strategy for all of us within our organization. My perfect TA department may not be your perfect TA department, but we can each build our own.

That's what's it all about, right? It's about us making the impact our organizations need, not about doing what someone else is doing. Sure, if you can "steal" some stuff that's working for someone else and it also works for you, well, that's working smart. But doing what everyone else is doing only because it worked for them is dumb and shortsighted.

You do you. Let others do themselves, and all of us trade, share, and steal ideas that we can test and try out in our environments until all the puzzle pieces fit in a way that's perfectly right for us.

In Chapter 1, I introduced the concept of "unicorns" in HR and talent acquisition. Google, in my mind, is the ultimate HR and TA unicorn. Laszlo Bock wrote a book in 2015 titled *Work Rules!* that many in our industry read and quote from like it's the Bible.

It is a rather good read, especially for us HR and talent nerds, but it's written from the perspective of a unicorn. Laszlo and the HR team at Google had almost unlimited resources and the top employment brand on the planet. It was a perfect petri dish for testing things out in HR and talent and seeing what might work.

If it didn't work, it was just "Google being Google." If it did work, it was "Oh, did you see what Google's doing? We need to do that!" Laszlo conceded in his book that after all the resources and time Google put into its TA function, Google was only 1 percent better than a coin flip in selecting talent.

Can you imagine? Basically, what Laszlo is telling us is that we would be much better off scrapping everything we do in talent acquisition, and inviting folks in that somewhat have the skills for the job, not interviewing, and then flipping a coin. "Heads, you get the job. Tails, you don't!"

This isn't an indictment of Google; it's an indictment of how extremely hard it is to hire the right talent for your organization. If the biggest unicorn in the world has a hard time hiring, we are all going to have a hard time hiring. I wish our executive teams understood what Laszlo understands. Then maybe more of us in TA and HR would get the resources we truly needed to build what they believe we should have.

So, we're not unicorns. I guess we just give up. I mean all the really good people will just go work for a unicorn. Did I mention that I hate victims?

We tend to have a victim mentality in TA and HR. Everyone else has it better. No one wants to work for us. Our pay sucks. Our benefits suck. Our managers suck. If you're a leader reading this, I want you to do yourself and your team a favor.

The next time you hear yourself or someone on your team being a victim, give them this "gift." Fire them. Yes, let them go.

Here's the reason this is a gift: We all should be able to experience the joy of working for something we truly believe in with all our hearts. Don't get this confused with "purpose-driven work." There's a big difference. You can be all-in with the company you work for without it being purpose driven.

The gift is working for an organization that you support and believe in. It's one of the strongest attributes you can have in talent acquisition, and I'll talk about this in detail in Chapter 6 when we start building our "perfect" TA team. If you or one of your team doesn't have this gift, go out and find it. It's a wonderful life to work for an organization where you are not a victim.

Sure, unicorns will have advantages we can't even imagine. Google posts a job and will receive thousands of applications within hours. You may wish you had that problem. But, let's be honest, it is a problem. Those thousands that are applying may be great candidates, but they're more likely not. Either way, the TA team has to work through the massive amount of activity to find the one "right" person.

I'm a true believer that while unicorns have many built-in advantages in talent acquisition, they're also severely limited in many ways, such as creativity. Facebook, another unicorn, can't go too crazy with its recruitment marketing because the brand is too big.

The media frenzy would be insane. While you can stand out on the corner in a Speedo swimsuit in your town with a sign that says, "Hiring More Folks Like Us!" and get a chuckle and some attention, Facebook would end up on the nightly news.

You can have some hiccups with your candidate experience and it won't make the news and become a social media disaster. Being smaller and nimble also has a unique set of advantages that unicorns wish they had.

Stop Doing Stuff That Doesn't Matter

The recruiting industry in general likes to poke fun at how corporate talent acquisition departments across the board struggle to do actual recruiting. It's mostly an unfair comparison between corporate talent acquisition and recruiters who work in an agency or Recruitment Process Outsourcing (RPO) environment. The agency/RPO recruiters only source and recruit. That's the sole job for which they get paid.

Can you imagine if your own corporate recruiting teams only had to recruit? In many cases, their capacity would easily triple, if not more.

This is the largest problem I see when I go into corporate talent acquisition shops and analyze their operations. Corporate talent acquisition does everything but talent acquisition. They go to meetings where someone believes talent acquisition should be present, but mostly it's a waste of time. They work on talent acquisition–related projects that are supposed to increase efficiency or increase quality or make interviewing easier or some other improvement. Mostly, these things never come to fruition. TA gets roped into community-related projects, massive organizational projects, and so on.

When I first joined Sparrow Health System in Lansing, Michigan, to run talent acquisition, I immediately could tell my team was in post-and-pray survival mode. Each recruiter was responsible for roughly one hundred or more requisitions. We were lucky to get jobs posted and pass on résumés and applications to hiring managers, let alone do anything else.

Something else I noticed was that my entire team was spending about 60 percent of their week in various meetings. Each meeting was *vital* for us to attend. I mean, we've been attending them for years. The departments we support *demand* we are at these meetings. We even run some of these meetings ourselves.

I find that the larger the organization, the higher the number of meetings you are forced to attend that are worthless. Can you imagine how much time is wasted at Walmart and Amazon? I love the old stories about Jack Welch at GE taking chairs out of conference rooms, forcing employees to stand throughout each meeting. Meetings certainly got much shorter during this experiment.

I blame Microsoft for corporate America's meeting obsession. Before Outlook calendar, we had significantly fewer one-hour meetings. As soon as people could easily, with one click of the button, schedule an hour on your calendar, our schedules got filled with one-hour meetings that really only have about ten minutes of content. But, if we're here for an hour, we may as well fill an hour!

At Sparrow, one of the first things I did was cancel all nonessential meetings my team was attending. Every single one. The only meetings we kept were the intake ones with hiring managers to discuss their openings, which were now mandatory for each opening, even openings that were frequent in nature. The team's full responsibility was now filling positions, only.

Was there fallout? Of course! Right away my team began coming to me with upset meeting owners wondering why talent acquisition and its new asshole leader weren't coming to their very important meetings. So, I told my team to schedule me in their place. I would attend each of these meetings and determine the importance of our attendance.

At these meetings, I spoke up, I got involved, asked some pointed questions about why I needed to be there, and what the specific purpose of this meeting was and whether it was still appropriate to have on a weekly or monthly basis. I probably ruffled some feathers. No one wants to be called out in their own meetings, but it was critical for the success of my team that I figure this out.

I explained that talent acquisition fails when we do things that are not about finding great talent for the organization. I had a go-to speech that sounded more like a sermon ready for each meeting about how these meetings were killing my team's ability to support the organization. Others chimed in with the same frustration about their teams and capacity as well.

It wasn't that we weren't willing, or wanting, to be a part of these meetings going forward; it was about finding out how we could increase the capacity of our teams, which they needed if we were going to do what our function was supposed to do for the organization.

Sometimes under the disguise of partnership, we do silly stuff like attend meetings that we really have no business being a part of, but leadership business wants to make sure everyone is involved and at the table. Welcome to the downfall of corporate America. I'm only half joking. Sure, we want to be a part of the business and a great partner, but sometimes this entire concept goes way beyond what it was originally designed to do.

Ultimately, we found that about 75 percent of the meetings we were attending weren't necessary for us to attend at all or all the time. We came to agreements with many meeting owners that any time they needed talent acquisition in the room, we would drop everything and attend, but as a normal course of business, we would not plan on attending. We kept abreast of what was happening in these meetings by continuing to be a part of the group email that had the meeting notes.

Another practice that I brought from my time at Applebee's was the fact we would not attend a meeting that didn't have a formal agenda for each meeting. I found that many of these ongoing weekly and monthly meetings had a standing agenda, which usually consisted of updates that were not worthy of a meeting. My team would not attend a meeting where a specific agenda was not sent out priorly.

The senior executive team loved this rule, and many instituted it as their own policy as well. If your meeting is important, then you should have an agenda of what's going to be presented, discussed, and decided upon. That way each of us can decide if it's critical we attend or not. It's just good, efficient business practice.

The perfect talent acquisition team is one that can do talent acquisition, not one that happily does everything but talent acquisition. It's unbelievable how fast you can fill forty hours a week with stuff, and then at the end of the week, realize none of it led to hiring great talent for your organization.

It's our job as talent acquisition leaders to eliminate distraction and increase the capacity of our teams to allow them to do what is most important—attracting and hiring talent. This must be your focus as a leader. No CEO ever said, "We have the best talent acquisition team on the planet because of all these great projects!" But, your team can't fill the openings your organization needs filled.

A great exercise to do with your team is list out everything you do individually and as a team, weekly and monthly within your roles, even the smallest details.[1] Then, as a group, force a certain percentage of this stuff to stop.

We will no longer set up interviews for hiring managers. Period.

What will happen? You will send out a notice to all the managers saying, "Going forward, talent acquisition will no longer play the third party to setting up interviews with candidates. It will now be the responsibility of the managers and their teams to do this task. We've found the process of being a go-between inefficient and it actually slows the process of bringing in candidates quickly."

About 3 percent of your managers will be completely pissed off by this memo, about 10 percent will applaud this change, and the rest won't care and have no issue either way.

Great talent acquisition happens when your team can do the actual recruiting they are hired to do. Another crazy thing will happen when you go on your capacity crusade. You're going to find out who on your team wants to recruit and who doesn't. As it turns out, some folks on your team don't really want to recruit. They love working in talent acquisition, they love getting paid, and they love the benefits, but they don't really like doing the hard work of recruiting, which is one reason you have this capacity issue to begin with.

If You Could Build Talent Acquisition All Over, What Would It Look Like?

I'll be honest, the reason we post and pray is that it's kind of how our entire function was designed when we were called the "personnel" department. Decades ago, if you worked in HR and had to hire people for your company, you would simply post the job internally, probably put a "help wanted" ad in the local paper, and that was the extent of your recruitment efforts. If you needed specially skilled people, you may attend some college career fairs or have an apprentice program, but there wasn't much more done to attract talent to organizations.

Recruiting talent today is very different in many ways, but the design of our departments in many cases hasn't changed from what it was thirty or forty years ago. Almost all TA departments are still housed under a traditional HR function. Most of us have one major piece of technology to support recruitment in our applicant tracking systems. We have recruiters whose job it is to find talent that is interested in our organization and our jobs. What if we blew up talent acquisition and started over with no memory of what it was before? Can you imagine finding a business leader from another planet who didn't have HR or talent acquisition to design a function that was responsible for increasing the talent in our organization? I'm 100 percent certain they would not come up with the current design, which begs the question, why do we continue to run talent acquisition like we do today?

I think our fictional outsider would look at the end result that needed to happen and think that this work looks very similar to what the marketing and sales team does in relation to attracting and closing clients. This work looks very similar to what the supply chain team does in relation to having the right amount of product and raw material at the right place at the right time. This work looks nothing like what HR teams do administratively to ensure our employees run like a well-oiled machine.

Fortunately, I do think we have many great examples currently taking place across the globe with organizations trying to disrupt the current talent acquisition model. Within the United States, Silicon Valley has added an exceptional amount of automation into talent acquisition over the last decade while trying to make it faster and more efficient.

If I was going to build a brand-new talent acquisition function from scratch, here are some ways I would change our function.

Make Talent Acquisition Part of the Marketing or Sales Department

Why? It's really the core function of great talent acquisition. Great TA starts with a brand: your employment brand. It's your story to candidates about why they would ever want to work for your company and in your jobs. Turns out, marketing departments are pretty good at this type of work.

Right now, in most organizations, marketing won't even give talent acquisition the time of day. They're busy trying to drive revenue for the organization. Admittedly, another extremely important function if we all want to have jobs. This leaves building an employment brand to people who, for the most part, don't have these skill sets.

Sure, in large, enterprise-sized organizations, employment branding is an entire department filled with talent who know how to do this. Most of us, though, will never have these skill sets at our disposal within talent acquisition and will have to rely on outside help or our own marketing teams with this work.

On the sales side of the business, they also have a unique set of skills that talent acquisition could greatly learn from. When you are hunting for candidates, not posting and praying, who are highly talented, they have many suitors. Salesmanship then becomes critical in winning the services of the top talent within your market.

There's an aspect of recruiting and sales that is one in the same. In sales and in recruiting, activity matters. If you make a hundred sales calls, you will get a result. Let's say that result is five completed orders of your product. If a salesperson needs to make ten completed orders, they know they need to make two hundred calls. To get to those two hundred calls, there are other activities, all of which lead to a traditional sales funnel.

Most modern talent acquisition departments today have this concept in play with the recruiting funnel shown in Figure 4–1.[2]

Like sales, you fill the top of the funnel with "prospects," or in our case candidates, then you work your way through the process to get to your end result. For sales, that's someone buying something from you. For talent acquisition, that's a candidate saying "yes" to our job offer.

Recruiting is just another variation of selling. Thus, having talent acquisition as part of your sales function, on many levels, makes complete sense, especially if you have a higher volume in recruiting.

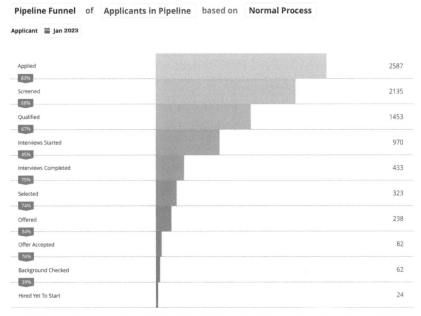

Figure 4–1. Recruiting Funnel

Understand That Design Matters

We live in a world where perception equals reality when it comes to candidate attraction. If you look old and stodgy, even though you're not, candidates will believe you're old and stodgy. You may be super conservative and have no modern qualities to your product, but your brand on the outside looks like the coolest thing on the planet, so candidates will want to come and work for you. Design matters in talent acquisition.

Of course, you always run the risk of not having your design match your culture, and this will cause premature turnover of candidates who will soon realize they were sold something that wasn't true. But the dirty little secret we all know, but don't talk about at parties, is there really isn't that much difference from one organization to the next. We're all racehorses and plow horses, not unicorns.

So, what do I mean when I say that design matters? Of course, there's an aspect of looking like a cool, modern organization on the outside to the candidates you want to attract. The best part about design is that the smaller you are, the easier this is to pull off, and it doesn't have to be super expensive. Giant brands have a much harder time doing this.

Have you ever looked at a Pottery Barn catalog? Don't you want your home to look just like those bright, airy, beautiful pictures in the catalog? So, you go buy the overpriced couch and super cool lamp, put it your dark, cramped living room and it looks nothing like the catalog. You want the design of your employment brand to look like the catalog, not your actual living room.

This isn't to say the design of your physical work environment isn't important. It's extremely important to a young workforce. They see pictures of the workspaces the unicorns have and they want that as well. They want the bright and cheery colors, modern work furniture, and standing desks. All of this matters to attracting great talent.

When someone comes to your organization to interview for a job and you have a 20-year-old couch with a coffee stain on it in the lobby, it sends an awful first impression. I know most organizations don't have the resources to do all these cool things, but you can do some stuff much cheaper than you think, and it makes a huge difference.

No one wants to work in an old musty office building with vertical blinds and beige walls. It feels like prison. The new talent acquisition understands the importance of design in everything we do in attracting top talent to our organization. Having great jobs at a great company with great pay is no longer enough. We now have to look the part as well.

People want to go to a job where they can post pictures on their social media accounts and be proud of the work environment, as much as the work they're doing. Is that a bit narcissistic? Yep, it is, and that's the reality of our current talent market. Ignore it, and your organization is on the outside looking in for the best talent.

Integrate Talent Acquisition into Your Business; Don't Bolt It On

Currently, talent acquisition is a separate function within your business. What if it wasn't? What if talent acquisition lived within each department, embedded as deeply as everything else that function was designed to do?

This point goes back to the concept that talent acquisition doesn't own recruiting; your hiring managers own recruiting. If a manager's most important function was increasing the talent of the team (attracting new great talent, developing current talent, driving performance, etc.), we would hire talent in our organizations much differently.

Of course, this sounds like eliminating talent acquisition as we know it and having each group or department do its own hiring. We are talking about the concept of how we would do talent acquisition if we started fresh. I use this example because it's the closest to reality we have. Frequently, when working with TA teams, I'll ask them, "What would happen to your organization if tomorrow your entire TA team was lost to some awful accident?"

Morbid thought, but stay with me!

Think about yourself and your own team. In reality, what would happen? The organization would mourn your loss, business would continue, there would be a scramble to fill your roles, and they would continue on. One other big thing would continue: hiring!

Wait, what? How could that be if we're all dead? That's the gut punch. Your hiring managers don't actually need you to hire someone for their team. They would figure it out. It would be clunky and slow, but in the interim, business would go on and managers would find talent in a number of ways to fill the openings they had.

I love this exercise with TA teams because it really puts in perspective what your true value is to the organization. In TA, we hire no one. Our entire job is to fill the top of the funnel with talent. If you can make your department understand that this is its job in the organization, you can make some great things happen.

Use Less Process and Make It Simple

I'm a huge fan of being process-driven as an organization, but those processes better be simple, or you're just part of the problem. Ironically, developing simple processes is harder than developing complex processes.

This is another major problem within many TA shops. We develop processes that help TA but don't necessarily add value to the rest of the organization. This is core issue in almost every function of the organization. We tend to develop policies based on the exceptions.

"Well, one time this thing happened, so we don't want that to ever happen again, so we will put a process in place to ensure that one thing never happens." Maybe that one thing really better never happen again, or maybe that one thing was a fluke and the chances it will ever happen again are so rare that this process is just a giant waste of time and resources. It's one of the primary reasons HR is believed to be so hated as a function—we process our organizations to death.

An example of a process I see often is with candidates. We need candidates to fill out certain aspects of our application, so we develop a process. If they don't follow this process, they won't be applicants, so we believe this will deter candidates from not following the process.

This works well for candidates who desperately want to work and have already made up their mind they want to work for you. But what about those candidates who don't even know you, or are maybe still on the fence but want to know more? Most TA shops disregard these candidates altogether when they are the candidates your hiring managers want most.

We put these types of processes in place because we don't want to deal with exceptions and set a precedent that you can fail to follow the process and still apply for a job. The reality is, we have hundreds of these types of processes in play at any one time in our organization, almost every single one not built with the candidate in mind, but built with our own interest in mind. How can I make my job easier in the long run? We need to make it easier for candidates now.

Be More Welcoming; Make Less of a Power Play

You know this was coming if you read the last section. Something really strange happened over the past fifty or so years. In HR and talent acquisition, we began treating people outside of our organizations who wanted to work for us like they were fortunate to even be able to communicate with us. In some organizations that I've seen, TA professionals basically talk down to candidates, forcing them to jump through hoops to even be considered.

Like it's some big privilege to work with your organization and a bunch of snobby people! I'm always perplexed when I run into these types of TAs, and I believe it's not that rare, unfortunately. It's your standard power trip. I'm working here, you're not, nana-nana boo-boo, I'm better than you.

It's childish, right?

Organizations should be the exact opposite. I know in TA, especially in popular companies, being wanted can be an exhausting job, but let me tell you, having the opposite problem is much worse. In a modern world, playing power trips on candidates will get found out and the negative reputation will spread like wildfire.

I love to take my grandmother's approach of treating others the way you want to be treated. You probably know this as the Golden Rule. It's simple, and it always works. Of course, we are talking Candidate Experience 101.

I was never a giant fan of the concept of candidate experience, probably because I've always been on the opposite side of the power play folks. My belief has always been that candidates' expectations are super low.

Basically, a candidate really only wants a few things. Tell me you got my résumé or application. Let me know if I'm a fit for the job, or if I'm not a fit. Let me know when that job has been filled. If you provide those three things, almost all candidates will think you did a pretty good job.

That's pretty simple, right? It's everything we would expect ourselves, and yet most organizations still don't do those three simple things. In fact, the 2016 Talent Board's report on candidate experience found that 47 percent of candidates were still waiting to hear back from employers more than two months after they applied.[3]

Two months? Almost half the candidates? Yeah, I don't think we have this figured out.

What's another place we are failing? Dispositioning, big time. From the report "What Candidates Want":

> After six years of candidate experience research, candidates still have one basic expectation of employers when it comes to screening: feedback and communication. Screening and dispositioning is one of the most intimidating aspects of the recruitment process as the majority of candidates do not get the job. Sixty-five percent of candidates receive no feedback after they are dispositioned and only 4 percent of candidates were asked for direct feedback during dispositioning.[4]

So, 65 percent of us are not telling candidates that we've selected someone else for the job. That's shameful of us, right?

The report doesn't say this directly, but there's one other thing at play in the candidate's perception of being told that they didn't get the job. If you're using your ATS to send an automated "thanks, but no thanks" message, the candidates aren't accepting this as you telling them. They want a real person—a recruiter or hiring manager, for example, to tell them directly. "Hey, Tim, it's Mary. Sorry, you did a good job, but we decided on another individual who fits what we were looking for a little more closely."

We hate making those calls, which is why 65 percent of candidates are telling us they didn't receive the call. Conflict avoidance is our downfall in talent acquisition. We hate making these calls because we know what's coming on the other end of the line. "Why didn't I get selected?" and, "What could I have done better?"

We hate those questions. We don't want to answer those questions. Either because we really don't know the answer, or we know the answer and it's tough to tell the candidate because it makes us feel awkward. "Yeah, well, Billy, quite frankly, you didn't have the project management experience at the same level as the other candidate we choose, so we decided to go that direction."

Seems simple enough, when you read the statement, but actually having that conversation with a person who may not be happy with the outcome isn't fun. It's like breaking up with someone. For sure, one side of that conversation is not going to be happy with the message. Maybe we should just disposition through text message. I'm kidding! Don't do that!

Be Data Driven in Talent Decisions

We still mostly use our gut when we hire talent. We lie to ourselves and say we factor in many pieces of data into each hiring decisions. We collect the behavioral interview decks from all those who interviewed, and we collect our personality assessment data, and if we're really strong, we have a work sample. But for the most part, we all sit around a table and ask, "So, who do you think?"

It's really hard to design a data-driven interview process. But I think if we were to start over in talent acquisition, we would rely quite a bit more on selection science. We would look at the cognitive ability of candidates, their ability to process information quickly, and their ability to learn new concepts. We would integrate work samples into all roles. We would design cultural assessments that ensure we better select candidates who actually want to work for an organization like ours.

It's not that we can't be better at interviewing. We can, but for the most part, we struggle in straight interviewing because we all have so many internal biases that it's just too much of a crapshoot. The one thing we know for sure is that we are more likely, in an interview process, to choose someone who is most like we are.

I'm a middle-aged white dude. If I interview another middle-aged white man, a young black woman, and an older white woman, I will most likely choose the other middle-aged white dude. Why? Because I'm racist or sexist? No, because I feel more "comfortable" with the other guy who is like me. We have more in common.

The same thing happens with every gender and every race. If you have a young black man interview three candidates, and one of those candidates is another young black man, he will almost always be chosen for the job. It isn't about race; it's about familiarity. They are more likely to have shared experiences where the decision maker will say, "I think I can really work with this person and do better work than with the other candidates."

This is why selection science is critical to hiring the best possible candidate for your organization. A human-driven process gets it right about 50 percent of the time. Each piece of nonsubjective data you can add to your process increases the likelihood that you will make better hiring decisions.

Stop Doing Giant Talent Acquisition Projects

The final thing I would suggest you do on the way to building a great talent acquisition department is to change your philosophy around projects. Most TA leaders and teams I meet have this giant laundry list of projects they want to get done. Almost every single person on the team is a "project lead" on a different project, each of which seem way too big to have multiple projects going on simultaneously.

I hate big, giant, fuzzy talent acquisition and HR projects. In my experience, I've seen way too many fail after weeks and months of effort and resources, and many times, these failures actually hurt people's careers with that company.

Here's the deal: no one wants your big, giant HR and TA project. Every part of your organization already has big, giant projects of their own to worry about, and they don't need HR and TA throwing another one on top, usually without any buy-in for those who have to do most of the work to make it a success.

"Hey, organization, it's us, TA, and today we are rolling out a brand-new hiring process in which you will now have to do twenty-seven new steps, learn to speak a never-before used form of the Japanese language, and learn to write in complete darkness. We are looking forward to working with you on this. If you have any questions please fill out the attached form and we'll get back to you within the next decade."

Then, we are totally and completely shocked our projects fail.

Instead, great TA shops never launch projects. Great TA teams take a page from software developers and they release alpha and beta tests. We find a single department or location and we test out things. This department has a leader who wants to champion this idea. More than likely, you've worked closely with this leader on a certain pain point and they are doing something different to help them out.

Sometimes these tests will fail. That's cool; it was only a test. We'll regroup, put something else together, maybe make some small changes, and test again. Sometimes, these tests are wildly successful. In that case, we can probably find another department or location who will want to beta the program as well. If it's successful again, pretty soon you'll have leaders knocking down your door to be the next one to test.

You can see what's happening, can't you?

No longer are you putting yourself in the role of big, giant failure of a project. Instead, you've changed the language of something we are going to do to you, to something we are doing for you for your specific group. Leaders love doing their own thing. In HR and TA, we can use that mentality to design great stuff that works, then slowly roll it out to locations and departments with leaders who want to get better.

What you'll find by making this change is that the weak leaders in your organization will start to stick out like sore thumbs. Those are the same leaders who worked to make sure your big, giant, fuzzy projects failed. Now, you've created a process in which you don't allow them to work against you; you only work with those leaders who want to work with you to succeed.

Eventually, those leaders who weren't supporting you will have to come to you for help because they'll see their peers doing this and having success. This ends up being much easier on your teams, puts much less stress on them, and actually puts them in a much better position of influence within the organization.

In reality, this testing method actually gets things done much faster in your organization as well. Executives are much more willing to test than allow you to spend big resources and make major changes that may fail.

Great talent acquisition is not about big changes. It's about continuously improving little by little over time. In real life, those who fail over and over don't end up succeeding; they end up giving up. It's the person who can build on small, daily successes that finds major success.

Here's the thing . . .

The only job of talent acquisition is to increase the talent in the organization. You do this by attracting talent to your organization. Don't make your processes and systems more complex than they need to be. Keep it simple and straightforward. The lighter your process is, the faster it can be. Talent acquisition departments need to be nimble and efficient. Stay laser-focused on adding value to the organization and candidates. Too often, average and below-average talent acquisition functions design things to make their lives easier, not candidates' lives.

» 5 «

Where Do We Even Begin?

This is really only a question a talent acquisition (TA) leader should ask themselves if one of the following scenarios is present:

- You're new to an organization and you need to overhaul or change the department.
- You've come from within the organization but not in TA and are taking over an existing function that you know is broken.
- You're developing a new function from scratch.

I don't think too many leaders would be asking where to begin if TA is running great and your organization is completely satisfied with the results.

I mentioned this earlier, but there's only one place to start. It's a question, a simple question, that most organizations fail to understand and support: Who owns TA?

It's a question the senior-most leaders have to answer, and they have to give you, the leader of talent acquisition, that answer. If you cannot get them to answer this question, run! Run away from the organization, because that is a position that is set up for failure from the very beginning.

I understand that this may be a cultural-shifting-type answer for most organizations, but it's the culture shift that is needed in today's highly competitive world for talent. As they say in the hit HBO television series *Game of Thrones*, "Winter is coming," and winter is coming for all organizations when it comes to finding talent.

I think I've said this enough that you know how important it is to get senior leadership on your side at the beginning. Once this buy-in happens and every manager knows they clearly own the staffing of their departments and teams, we can get down to the business of truly supporting them with a world-class recruiting function.

It's important to note, once again, that saying out loud, especially when you're new to an organization or function, that you don't want to own it will really make some leaders take pause. It's critical for your survival and influence that you are prepared with a detailed explanation of why this philosophy is so important to the success of attracting talent to your organization.

Recruiting is not something that one function can do effectively in any organization. When Hillary Clinton was first lady of the United States, she wrote a book on society's role in protecting children titled *It Takes a Village*.[1] Talent acquisition takes a village. It takes every single person in your organization working together, constantly, to win.

Organizations for decades have been using this concept for customer service. We are now seeing the top organizations in the world use this philosophy when it comes to attracting talent and providing exceptional candidate experience. This doesn't mean everyone "owns" recruitment. Everyone owning recruitment is also a failing proposition.

There's a psychological phenomenon that happens when people see a car wreck. We see this phenomenon in action on our commutes to and from work on the highway. A car wreck happens and hundreds of cars will pass by without stopping to help.

If that car wreck happened on a rural road or at night with fewer cars around, someone driving by would almost always stop and help. If others are around, we assume someone else will help, so we take on less ownership. We tell ourselves, "I'm busy, there are others here, someone else will stop and help."

When we stumble on the same event by ourselves, we take on full ownership by stopping and doing whatever we can to help those involved. The psychology behind this is the same in organizations when we try and say, "It's everyone's responsibility," for anything.

If everyone is responsible, then no one is responsible.

We need everyone to be involved in attracting and recruiting talent to the organization, but one person should own it, the hiring manager, and one person should be responsible for making sure the activity happens, the head of talent acquisition, or whatever the title is at your organization.

If you can start at this place, your life as a leader of talent acquisition will be in a wonderful place, no matter what else you may be challenged within your organization.

If All Else Fails, Do What's Important

Corporate HR will remain one of the most hated functions if it continues to do what keeps it busy, instead of what is most important. It's why employees, in general, get so frustrated with the HR function. HR tends to let the process run them; they don't run the process. Talent acquisition must break this cycle.

Mel Robbins, author of *The 5 Second Rule: Transform Your Life, Work, and Confidence with Everyday Courage*, shares the following chart I love to use when explaining how you should prioritize all the things that come your way on daily basis (Figure 5–1).[2]

In talent acquisition, we are constantly being told every opening is "urgent." I'm not saying that every opening is not urgent in your

	Urgent	Not Urgent
Important	Do It Now	Plan It
Not Important	Do or Delegate	Drop It

Figure 5–1. Prioritizing Daily Tasks

organization. If you ever work in a startup environment, you quickly find out how urgent every opening truly is.

When we add in importance we begin to see where our priorities must be directed. Every hiring manager will tell you how important their openings are to the team's and the organization's success. Rarely does a talent acquisition department have enough resources to make everyone happy.

Great talent acquisition leaders prioritize the workload for their teams well. They are able to go to a high organizational level and see what work is important and urgent, and what work is important but not as urgent. The rest of the work gets delegated back to the department from which it came, or it gets dropped altogether, with a quick explanation of why it's being dropped. Never leave work undone without telling those who expect it to be done why you and your team won't be doing it.

The best way I've seen TA leaders decide what is important and urgent is to get all the parties involved who believe their work is the most important and urgent along with a senior leader or two who are ultimately responsible for all the involved parties. These meetings do not take long, and everyone leaves with a clear understanding of what will happen next.

If the TA leader comes in with all the options and possibilities that can be realistically managed, those in the room will pretty quickly decide among themselves which situations are urgent and important. It helps to have their superiors in the room.

You should never have a meeting where all the work is deemed important and urgent and you just have to find a way to make it happen. That is not a solution. That is not managers owning the problem. One solution may be, "We've decided as a group all of this work is important and urgent, and to ensure you can accomplish this work successfully, we are going to give you additional resources."

I'm always happy with that outcome. I love additional resources!

I will refuse to leave the room if the outcome is, "do more with less." That is an outcome of failure for all involved, not just you. You need to get something for your team—more resources, more time, a change in scope, and so on. Talent acquisition should be the experts in negotiation in your organization. This is when those negotiation skills are best used.

Right about now, if I were you, I would be asking myself, "Okay, I get it. Do what's important and urgent. But really, what are the most important things to do first?"

Talent acquisition is about finding talent and filling positions. If you want to start somewhere, filling open positions is a great place to start, right? This is also a big trap.

Remember at the beginning of this chapter, I said there are really only three types of TA leaders who need to know where to start? Those who are new at the organization, new to the role, or new to function. Just starting to fill positions is the fastest way to failure if you and your team are not prepared to fill positions.

Don't get me wrong. Anyone can fill an opening in your company. We aren't launching the space shuttle; we're just finding some folks who may make good employees. But that work of finding good employees never stops. The first week I became a recruiter, my boss told me, "The best thing about filling those positions is they'll always be there tomorrow," and he was right. In twenty-five years, I've never had a time, even during the Great Recession, that I didn't have at least one position that needed to be filled.

The first thing you need to do is figure out what your function will be, and how the organization will view you.

Always Be Yourself. Unless You Can Be a Unicorn, Then Always Be a Unicorn!

HR professionals may have low self-esteem because they have allowed other functions and employees to knock them down. Sales, as a function, doesn't have low self-esteem. In fact, it's the opposite. Operations, as a function, doesn't have low self-esteem. Low self-esteem functions have very little influence in an organization. Talent acquisition cannot have low self-esteem.

One of the first steps to becoming truly great in talent acquisition is changing the perception of talent acquisition within the organization. You do this by doing things differently than they were done before, or at least giving the perception to the organization that things are being done differently, through your words and actions.

This doesn't mean you're going to go out and lie about what TA is doing. This means TA will go out and become very public within the organization about marketing what they are doing. You are going from whatever your current-state TA function is to a "talent advisor" talent acquisition function.

What the heck is a talent advisor?

Talent advisors have a number of different titles. On the HR side of the house, these are your true HR business partners. On the TA side, organizations may call them a talent acquisition consultant, recruiting consultant, talent acquisition partner, talent acquisition specialist, or talent management advisor, to name a few.

A talent advisor is a recruiting professional who is not an order taker, but a talent acquisition professional who influences hiring decisions. They gain this right to influence by adding to the staffing decision equation with acute knowledge of the organization, expertise of external markets, and keen insight of the business.

CEB Global estimates that only about 20 percent of all corporate talent acquisition professionals are at the consultant-type level of a talent advisor. The key to becoming a talent advisor is your ability to act in a consultative role with your hiring managers. You become an equal, if not greater part, of influencing who is hired and why.

Talent advisors are the organization's experts when it comes to attracting and hiring the right talent. Just as a lawyer is your organization's expert in legal matters, your team of talent advisors are your internal experts on talent and hiring. Hiring managers begin to rely on the advice of talent advisors, as they do from other key influencers within your organization.

How does one become a talent advisor? This is a huge part of how you begin to set up your function to run as a leader (Figure 5–2).[3] The biggest piece of having your team become talent advisors is about you as a leader, defining what a talent advisor means to you and the organization, and setting the expectation of how your team will perform in that role moving forward, and of course, developing your team to become talent advisors.

The Talent Advisor Capability Model

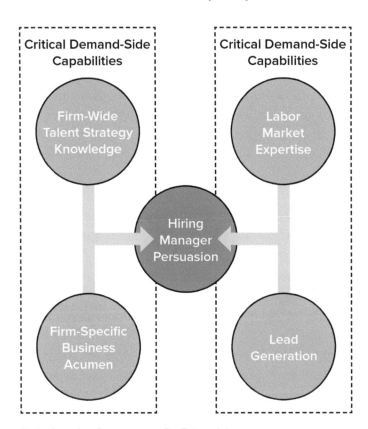

Figure 5–2. Develop Recruiters to Be Talent Advisors

I'll talk more about who should be on your team, making it easier to deliver on your promise of being talent advisor, in the next chapter. But first, we need to lay out how to design your function around this concept of becoming a talent consultant to the organization. There are definitely some strategies you will need to implement to help your chances of success:

Design and/or Overhaul Your Job Requisition Intake Process

Traditionally, in most organizations, the hiring manager gets approval for an opening. They email the recruiter supporting their department the details, which is usually some outdated job description written ten years ago and doesn't even come close to the actual current job or responsibilities. The recruiter then posts the job within the system and begins working on it.

Sound about right?

An intake process (many people call these meetings) is a set of questions and conversations that take place to ensure both the hiring manager and the recruiting team are on the same page of what is needed, so that no resources or time are wasted. This process is designed to deliver the best candidate experience possible, as well as find the most talented candidate possible that fits within the specifications the organization has decided are needed.

It's helpful to have a specific agenda for each of these intake meetings so that no pieces are missed, and every question is asked and answered. I want my intake process to have consistency and value for all parties involved. This process is done for every single opening, even openings that you will fill more than once in a year.

Some hiring managers find that last point annoying. Why do we have to have this meeting to fill a call center rep position? We just had this exact opening last month.

Is it truly the *exact* opening? Did you find the *perfect* person last time, or were there some concessions? Will there be concessions this time? Are there certain skills that your team is weak on right now that this hire may be able to fill? What is the status of your succession pipeline?

Do you see where this is going? Each opening is unique. Granted, you will have some openings that you fill quite often, but I still recommend that my talent advisors get in front of the hiring manager frequently to game plan and brainstorm. That's what consultants do: they offer their expertise, and then continue to offer their expertise. They don't offer it once, then never come back, and feel like they're truly being supportive.

Involve the Hiring Team in the Sourcing Process

I go beyond just the hiring manager because, remember, it takes a village. Our reality is that the incoming team this new hire will work with probably has a better network than your hiring managers. Most hiring managers are in their position because they have tenure with one organization, so their networks aren't as active as rank-and-file employees.

Employee referrals are usually in the top three of highest source of hires for all organizations, and usually, at the top when it comes to quality of hire. Activating the hiring team in the sourcing process is critical to success.

A strategy I've seen, especially in the startup world, is for talent acquisition teams to schedule a sourcing activity with all the hiring team members, hiring manager, talent advisor, and all department teammates. With everyone together, we ask, "Who do we know or are connected to that we can somehow engage?"

Everyone gets out their laptops and starts going through their connections on Facebook, LinkedIn, X (formerly known as Twitter), their church directory, and their kid's soccer parent roster. We look anywhere and at anyone to find the talent we need. It's actually a pretty cool and fun way to source and you get some great information from the team on what companies have great reputations, which ones they would hate to work for, and so on.

I also pick up a ton of valuable candidates for other positions we have open or will have open eventually. The teams don't think like we do. When one team member makes a comment like, "Oh, Ted, he was the best finance guy I've ever worked for," I'm making a mental note, and physical note, to connect with Ted. I may not have an opening right now, but when I do, I have a potential rock star in waiting. That's thinking like a talent advisor.

Always Be Switzerland

Great consultants are great consultants because they always tell you what you need to hear in a way you will accept and that doesn't make you feel defensive. How? The hiring manager always feels that you 100 percent have their best interest in mind, and only their best interest. It just happens to be that their best interest will also be the organization's best interest.

One way I would train my team in becoming effective talent advisors is to always come across as supportive to all the other functions, especially to HR. That reputation of being supportive to all is a positive trait in organizations, and we know our brothers and sisters in HR get beat up on too often.

If we can provide a united front and help HR, it will just make everything we do in TA that much easier. Plus, if your team excels at being talent advisors, your influence will increase rapidly in the organization, and others will follow your lead in supporting each other. That's a great culture to work in, and one we would all enjoy.

Belief and Perception Happen Faster with Good Marketing

The belief and perception of your team currently may be that you aren't very good at recruiting. Perception becomes reality. We need to change the organization's perception by saying that recruiting is now different, and better than ever before. That we've become world class and are using the same technology and process as industry-leading talent acquisition shops.

This messaging within the organization is critical in changing how the organization speaks about talent acquisition both internally and externally. Your team has to be able to share this messaging in everything they do in their normal course of business conversations. They must walk the walk, so to speak.

Great talent acquisition happens through great leadership, great talent, great accountability, and, whether we like it or not, some good old-fashioned marketing of what you are actually doing.

Unicorn TA shops are great at this. I can't even tell you how many conference sessions I've sat in and listened to a unicorn TA leader spout off about some great thing they're doing to change the world of TA and it's something most organizations have been doing as a best practice for five years. But, the room is packed to hear how Google is doing whatever it is they're doing.

By the way, most of internal cultures are built the same way. Of course, you need all the great components of a great culture, but you also need to keep telling your teams you have a great culture. You could have all the components in place and never talk about it and most employees would say the culture is just "normal" when asked.

Marketing Is a Powerful Drug

I frequently see talent advisor–led TA teams going through internal team branding exercises because they understand the power of having a "TA brand" in the scope of how the organization perceives your abilities as a team. In the end, you still have to perform, but if you know you are performing or can perform, changing the narrative of your team across the organization can do wonders for team dynamics.

In 2016, Nellie Peshkov, vice president of talent acquisition at Netflix, took the stage at LinkedIn's Talent Connect Conference and explained to the crowd how Netflix creates a partnership between hiring managers and recruiters, internally. Peshkov had seven elements to share:[4]

1. **Train hiring managers to help unearth new talent.** Like my example above in startups, it's important to not only ask for help in sourcing but actually show hiring managers how it's done.
2. **Ask a lot of questions.** This goes back to designing the right intake process, but it also goes a bit deeper than just a form. I call this the "jealous spouse" theory of questioning. If I came home late one night and smelled of perfume, I would expect my wife would ask me a litany of questions, and even after I gave her answers, she would ask follow-up questions, and it probably wouldn't stop until she was exhausted. Recruiters need to be a jealous spouse when questioning hiring managers about a job. If something doesn't seem right, ask the question. When in doubt, ask the question. Something doesn't make sense. Ask. The. Question.
3. **Don't wait to give feedback and advice to your hiring managers.** Okay, first let's make sure you understand that advice better be talent acquisition related, to begin with. You're the TA expert, so this is your place to give advice. If you build a great relationship with this manager then down the road maybe you can give leadership and operational advice. Talent advisors don't wait to be asked for TA advice. You're paid to be an expert, and experts give advice in places they feel they can help.

4. **Raise the talent bar.** I'll share more in Chapter 6, but understand who on your team needs to go away, and who on your team has the talent to do the job of a talent advisor.

5. **Stay on top of talent acquisition trends and continually work to improve.** I'm a TA tech junkie and can't get enough of it. I understand most people in recruiting are not as geeky as I am. Great talent acquisition happens at the fringes. Keeping up to date with the latest trends of what's going on in talent acquisition is definitely part of the job description of a talent advisor. The other aspect of this is how hiring managers will gain respect for your expertise. If you are constantly talking to them about ideas and trends, they will have confidence that they are in good hands because people who stay on top of their profession are more likely to want to perform that profession at a higher level.

6. **Make yourself a member of the "circle of trust."** I have a small crew of professional folks in my circle of trust. I can tell them anything, ask any question, and there will no judgment, only help and advisement. Hiring managers have a circle of trust and you need to find a way to get in that circle and become their trusted advisor. This takes time and you usually have limited opportunity to prove yourself, so don't miss your chances and don't fail.

7. **Live your TA vision.** If you don't have confidence in yourself and your team, no one else will. Your vision may not be the best, but if you have confidence in it and get others to believe in it, you can make great things happen. To do this, you have to be 100 percent completely bought in and live your vision every day.

Always Say Yes

In HR and talent acquisition, we need to change our language. Actually, we need to change one word we use way too often: "No." It's our go-to word across the vast function of human resources. If you were to ask employees to give you one word to explain HR, that word would be "no."

Great talent acquisition starts with a "yes." Don't think I'm blindly asking you to start saying "yes" to every request some hiring manager or department is asking of you. Being customer service–focused in HR and TA is what got us into this mess. "The customer is always right" is one big giant lie.

When I hear a leader say, "You need to be more customer-focused, and I'm your customer," what I'm really hearing is, "Do what I say because I'm the customer, and the customer is always right." Well, you're not my customer. We're partners in this nightmare you've created, so put a helmet on because things are about to get real.

A funny thing happens when you say "no" to someone, especially someone who already is coming to you with a preconceived notion that you'll say "no." It's a physical reaction that you can actually witness in real time. Here's how it typically plays out:

> *Hiring Manager:* "Hey, Tim, I wanted to run something by you. We've been struggling to hire some good people, and I think I've got an idea that could help. My brother's boy is just getting out of prison and, well, he didn't do anything really bad, and I know the kid, and I know he's a good worker. I want to hire him. What do you say?"
>
> *Me (Playing the role of a bad TA leader):* "No. You're an idiot!" (Okay, I didn't really say "you're an idiot" out loud, that was my internal voice. I just said, "No!")
>
> *Hiring Manager (Shoulders drop, head drops slightly, exhales breath):* "Okay, I didn't think so but wanted to check; we could really use the help."

You've seen this physical reaction when you've told someone "no," haven't you? I see it with my kids constantly, and it's no different in a professional setting. Hunched over, backing away from you, depression almost setting in.

It's rare that we even get an employee or manager to come see us, and if our first reaction is "no," the chance they will come back to see us is almost zero. Let's take the exact same scenario above, but use "yes" instead:

> *Hiring Manager:* "Hey, Tim, I wanted to run something by you. We've been struggling to hire some good people, and I think I've got an idea that could help. My brother's boy is just getting out of prison and, well, he didn't do anything really bad, and I know the kid, and I know he's a good worker. I want to hire him. What do you say?"

> *Me (Playing the role of a good TA leader):* "Sounds like you're thinking outside the box. I like it. I'm going to say "yes."

> *Hiring Manager (Picking up jaw off the floor, head up, eye contact, coming toward me):* "Wow! I didn't expect that. Don't we have rules around hiring people with records? I thought you'd say no, but I wanted to check because I really do think he'll do well."

> *Me (Now playing the role of a great TA leader):* "There will be some challenges for sure, and we'll have to get sign-offs from some higher-ups. They will probably want your guarantee on this one."

> *Hiring Manager:* "Guarantee?" (*Head moving side to side like when you ask your dog who is the better presidential candidate.*)

> *Me (Becoming a talent advisor):* "Well, not a real guarantee, but this hire will follow you. This is risky, and you're asking for permission to do it. If it doesn't work out. . . . You know what? I can always say no, and then it's not your problem any longer. Then it's on me. It's also on me to find you some real candidates that won't be as risky. It's your call. How can I help?"

The "yes" turned this from a negative "you-always-tell-me-no, I-hate-HR" conversation to a "You definitely have a valid concern" conversation. The hiring manager sees me working hard to solve his problem, that I'm the person to help solve that problem, and I have his back.

From "No" to "Yes"

One of those words stops the conversation. One will open up the conversation and begin a partnership. Great talent acquisition and the talent advisor persona are built on relationships that become partnerships, and those don't happen without genuine open and honest conversations.

Read through the "yes" conversation again. Not one thing I said was a lie or fabrication. I was honest. I was trying to work with the manager to solve a problem and put that manager in the best light possible within the organization. That manager will come back to me again and ask for help. Saying "no" could have ended that conversation quickly and probably ensured that I never had this manager come to me with an issue again. Many in our industry choose to just say "no" because it's easier.

The Fine Line between Great Leader and Friend

Like everyone, I want to be a great leader. Like any leader, I think the definition of great is dependent on who is listening to your message, and what they take away from that message. Leaders are constantly asked to walk a fine line between doing what is right for the business and doing what is right for our employees.

As most of you know, these two things don't go in opposite directions but instead run parallel in the same direction, although many times, our employees don't feel these are traveling in the same direction. It's not one or the other, business versus employees; it's both.

You need the both groups to be healthy; one can't live without the other. Although I think both bad leaders and average employees believe they can survive without the other.

What I've learned from watching both great leaders and bad leaders is that your ability to walk that fine line successfully determines your fate. It's a very small margin for error. You must be fair, consistent, and above all, communicate in an upfront, transparent way when you can.

Before I was put into a leadership position I didn't get this fine line. I would be frustrated with my leaders. Why didn't they support us more?

Why did they seemingly always support the business? I vowed, when I was a leader, I'd be the person they didn't have the courage to be.

It's funny how careers have a way of giving you what you ask for.

The best TA leader I ever worked for gave me some advice, and frequently, I've reached back for it. He said, "Tim, employees will never throw you a party when you take something away. But if it is the right thing to do, then you have to do it. Because they will throw you a going-away party when you get fired for not doing the right thing."

He wanted to know if I wanted to be the kind of leader that employees wanted to throw a party for, or the kind of leader that employees didn't want to throw a party for. Meaning, do what's right for the business when that's what is called for. Those who don't understand will never understand, so don't worry about what they think.

A piece of being a great leader is having blinders on to all the noise. As a leader in talent acquisition, you will have never-ending noise. The TA leaders who are most successful figure out ways to lessen the noise, overall, but also ensure the right noise is amplified.

As a new TA leader in an organization, don't allow negative noise to continue without swiftly addressing it at the source. The great thing about organizations is there's always a trail to follow, and leaders don't have to do this often if individuals know it will happen.

One of the hardest parts of taking over a TA function is that your own team members are usually the largest noisemakers. Before you came, their world was perfect. Post and pray. Come in at 8 a.m., leave by 4 p.m., no pressure, no worries, nice check and benefits.

When I'm asked, "What are the first things new TA leaders need to do?" quite frankly it involves getting rid of some of their own team. I rarely find a broken TA department that is completely filled with well-meaning, highly skilled recruiters who just happen to need some "leadershipping."

I didn't start the chapter with "your team sucks and they need to be fired" because I don't think anyone takes a job or that we hire anyone thinking they will suck. This is just one component of many you'll have to address, and the next chapter is designed to help you with this specific issue.

Here's the thing . . .

If your hiring managers are not bought into the fact that they own the talent on their teams, you will be fighting an uphill battle your entire existence with your organization. Fight this battle. Win this battle. It's a key differentiator of great talent acquisition leaders. Never let up on this ideal. The only job of a hiring manager is to increase the talent on their teams. This is how TA supports the organization. This is the synergy that is needed for world-class talent acquisition.

» 6 «

A Talent Acquisition Leader Is a Dealer in Hope

O kay, the reality is every leader is a dealer in hope, but I feel it's especially true when you talk about talent acquisition. Our entire function is predicated on us bringing in new talent to the organization—the talent we hope will help us succeed and grow. We truly have no idea if they will or not (remember Google's 1 percent better example?).

In this chapter, we'll look at how a great talent acquisition leader builds their team from the ground up. That's easy to do if you're starting from scratch and it's a little harder when you take over a team, but either way, you can start to collect and develop the skill sets and personalities your team needs to be successful.

Every hire we make as a leader is hopeful. We hope that they perform at a high level. Our expectations for what someone can and will do are usually off-the-charts high, when ultimately, we should expect just average. We never do; we expect exceptional, and it rarely shows up. If someone performs average, we believe we failed in a hire, which makes no sense, but it all comes back to those insane expectations we place on new hires.

We hope for great and we usually get average. About 10 percent of the time we'll get great, and about 10 percent of the time we'll get bad.

The organization doesn't really know the difference of performance when it comes to average and great recruiting. Almost all organizations are on a scale of average to below average in terms of overall recruiting ability so most leaders and managers have never even seen or heard of great recruiting.

Many times, when you show them what great recruiting is, they will confuse it for bad recruiting because it's so different from what they've experienced in the past. Great recruiting to a hiring manager is more work for them than bad recruiting. In bad recruiting, the manager just sits back and waits for you to deliver talent. In great recruiting, a hiring manager is actively involved in recruiting talent for their team. See how this can be easily misinterpreted by a hiring manager?

We've conditioned our recruiting teams in the same manner. Most corporate talent acquisition professionals believe it's their job to deliver talent to hiring managers. They believe this is "great customer service" and what the hiring manager actually wants. So, great recruiting teams start with a re-education about the truth.

The truth is everything we've been talking about up to this point. It's realignment of ownership and responsibility. It's taking a look at talent from a strategic point of view, not a tactical point of view. Great recruiting teams all share a certain DNA, so to speak. One segment of that DNA is a leader, you, who gets it, who flat out understands the effect of talent on your business and how to deliver what the organization needs in a way that is sustainable over a long period of time.

I'll be honest, with enough resources and sheer will, any idiot can produce short-term talent acquisition results. It takes a talent acquisition leader with vision and plans to sustain that success over an extended time frame. Strategic versus tactical is how this is usually perceived.

Great talent acquisition is both strategic *and* tactical, not one or the other. You need great strategy and great tactical ability to sustain long-term success. Strategy without tactics is just a good preacher story on a Sunday morning. Tactics without strategy are just motion for the sake of motions.

Do the People You Hire in Talent Acquisition Scare You?

I have a strong belief about HR and talent acquisition that I learned from a CEO mentor in my career. That belief is that we generally under-hire talent when filling openings on our teams. We hire people we know are less talented than we are. We hire people who won't push us out of our comfort zone.

On one of my career stops, I ran into this scenario and it's the clearest example I can share. I came into the HR team at a director-level role running talent acquisition. I had four other director-level peers on the HR team, and we all worked closely together.

One of those directors had been with the organization going on twenty years. She started in the organization as a receptionist. "Tim," the CEO told me, "this is Mary [not her real name]. She's the director of HR, and she started with us as the 'front-desk girl.'"

As a receptionist, Mary did awesome, so well that when the HR secretary position came open, Mary was asked to fill it. She did great as the HR secretary, and when an employee relations representative position came open, she applied for and got that job.

From employee relations representative, she was promoted to senior employee relations representative, and then down the road, she was promoted to manager of employee relations. Eventually, her director retired and she moved into the director role where she had been for the past seven or eight years.

Good for her. Great performance and tenure are rewarded.

The problem was, the CEO didn't see her as a "director" within his HR team. He saw her as the "front-desk girl," and he was very proud to share this story with many people in what he thought was a perfect story of loyalty and promotion from within the organization—although he had little respect for anything she had to say.

You could easily say this is the CEO's problem. For sure, part of it is. But it also points out a global epidemic we have in HR that you don't see in many other functions within our organizations. We tend to hire down, not up. We take the easy route.

We don't hire people who scare us.

We don't hire people who are so freaking smart and talented that we worry one day they will take our job and rise above us. We don't hire people who are better than we are, and our executives know this.

When was the last time one of your HR or TA colleagues was promoted into a leadership role in another function within your organization?

Almost never do we see this happen. But we frequently see people promoted from outside of HR and TA into leadership roles in our function.

My one criterion for hiring in HR and TA is simply this:

Does the person scare the bejesus out of you?

Is the person so talented, smart, and ambitious that you know one day you will probably be reporting to them? Are they better than you?

When I went to work at Applebee's in HR, I was surrounded by people who were talented. Applebee's, and the head of HR, Lou Kaucic, over-hired when it came to HR. People on the team came from Disney, General Electric (GE), and other organizations known for stellar HR.

Kaucic knew Applebee's wasn't just cold beer and good burgers. Any chain could produce those things consistently. It was about hiring and developing a better workforce. That could not easily be replicated by another casual dining competitor, and the only way you get there is to have industry-leading HR talent and practices. The day I interviewed with Applebee's it took eight hours. My future boss, Jackie Giusti, was former military police and a trained interrogator. It was unlike any HR interview I had ever been a part of because it all came down to one thing.

Jackie only had one measure she wanted interviewees to live up to when making a hiring decision for her team, and it was the last question she asked me at dinner, eight hours into the interview:

"Are you better than me?"

As a candidate sitting across the table being asked that question, you have limited options. You can say you are better, you can say you're not better, or you can say some middle-of-the-road answer that is really just a nonanswer. After eight hours of being interrogated, I knew the nonanswer would not fly with Jackie.

So, I said what I felt: "Yes, I'm better than you."

I then looked hopefully for some sort of facial cue that would allow me to explain. Yes, I was better in certain aspects of HR and talent acquisition. My experience to that point gave me a few tools in the shed she may not have yet. Of course, there were things I could learn from her, but there were also things I could teach her.

Luckily, my first answer was a winner. She explained that the only way would have hired me was if I was better than she was, and in her mind, she needed to hear it and believe it. She could only hire noticeably better talent into HR and TA. I don't think I let her down, although truthfully, the team probably taught me more than I was ever able to teach them.

I don't think I scared Jackie. I don't think anything scares Jackie. But the Applebee's process taught me how important it is to hire better talent into HR and TA. I never was talked down to by other employees at Applebee's from other functions like I have been in almost every other stop in my career. The organization respected the noticeably better talent and what it could bring to helping them run great restaurants, and we delivered.

The first step to building a great talent acquisition team is hiring people who scare you—in a good way.

How to Hire a Perfect Talent Acquisition Professional

At some point in almost every single talent acquisition leader's career, you will have to hire someone onto your team. For most of us, this scenario will happen hundreds of times throughout our career. Each hire is an opportunity. We are supposed to be the experts in hiring, so it's even more critical for us to get this right.

Carmen Di Rito, cofounder and chief development officer at LifeCo UnLtd in Johannesburg, South Africa, wrote a brilliant piece on team selection for leaders that looked at seven specific components a leader should consider before hiring. I love these because hiring great talent is less about selection and more about the preparation you put in to put yourself in the right position to make a great selection. Here are Di Rito's seven components:[1]

1. **Look for attitude alignment.** When recruiting for a new position in talent acquisition, it is more important to look for alignment in thinking than competency and expertise. I can teach anyone to recruit, but if I'm spending all my time trying to get them to think differently, I'm in trouble. Changing someone's core belief about how they do something, especially in adult learners, is extremely hard. It's one reason so many experienced recruiters fail at a new position when they were successful at their last position: lack of attitude alignment.

2. **Be fanatical.** As a talent acquisition leader, you need to fixate on building a cohesive and robust team that believes in and lives your values. This creates a culture that you are all proud of and enjoy being around. This was Lou and Jackie from Applebee's. Strong cultures beat weak cultures. You only build a strong culture by being a fanatical leader.

3. **Be brutally honest.** Have you ever interviewed a candidate and spent most of the time trying to talk him out of the job? You were being brutally honest in hopes that if you did this, the ones who couldn't handle it would self-select out of the process. If you want to get great talent on your team, you need to share the greatest frustrations and challenges up front. No sugarcoating. This is being authentic at a much higher level than your employment brand.

   Our employment brand is the best version of us. It's honest without sharing our worst days. We all have bad days, but we have more great days. This is really how employment brand transparency plays out. Great teams are not built on our best days; they're built on our worst, and they still want us on our worst days.

   The one problem with being brutally honest is that most employees can't take it. We all say we want honesty and then someone tells us that our baby is ugly and we no longer want honesty. To become a leader who can be brutally honest, it must start at the interview stage. You have to let those who may come into your organization know that brutal honesty is part of the deal. They need to be warned.

You need to warn them that for the first time in their entire career they will be given brutally honest feedback, and it will sting. Sometimes it will hurt, and they will want to fight back and react, but that's not the reaction they should have. In the interview is where you train your future hires that delivering brutally honest feedback is about developing them to be their best. That the only thing you're trying to do, the only thing you even care about, is helping them become better.

It's all about L.O.V.E. The best feedback I ever saw delivered was by the legendary King of Pop, Michael Jackson. When preparing for his last tour, right before his death, he was giving some feedback to his musicians. They weren't doing something the way he wanted. Jackson was famously shy, quiet, and polite, but when it came to *his* performance, he was unbending on his expectations. He was brutally honest with the musician and then said, "It's all about love. L.O.V.E." I'm going to tell you exactly what you need to hear, but only because I care about you being the best.

The leader who can get to this point in their career has truly reached a different level.

4. **Develop a compelling, audacious vision.** Do you want a vision that will attract people who are courageous, tenacious, and hardworking? Well, that sounds easy. Ugh! It's really hard, but when you get it right, it's such a great tool to help you build a great team. People want to work for a leader with a great vision. We all have a great vision inside of us; it's just that sometimes it's really difficult to put that vision into words that will drive passion.

   My advice is that you should have a talent acquisition function vision that is different from the organizational vision. It should be something that your entire team remembers and can easily recite to anyone. The best visions are ones that your hiring managers will know as well. This means it probably should be fewer than seven or so words.

At my own company, HRU Technical Resources, we developed an organizational vision years ago. It was four sentences, which were almost paragraphs by themselves. It wasn't a vision that inspired or was one anyone could remember. My recruiting team is high functioning and high volume, and they came up with their own: "We put asses in seats!"

It's funny, it's easily remembered, and it's audacious. The only problem I had was it didn't speak to quality. I just didn't want any ass in a seat; I wanted our clients to know we only recruited great talent. So, we made one small adjustment to our vision: "We put great asses in seats!" There, that's better!

5. **Disrupt.** I hate best practices! Doesn't that sound ridiculous? Who hates best practices? Best practices are the industry standard for what works; no one hates best practices. I do.

Best practices are basically something someone came up with years ago. They took this idea and implemented it. It worked, so they kept doing it. Eventually, others heard of this idea and they also tried it. It worked for them as well. Eventually, it became a best practice.

Great. Let's do something in our own shop that was "innovative" years ago and now everyone is doing it. Does that sound disruptive? No. It sounds like you're a follower. I want innovation. I want to be the starter of best practices. I don't want to follow best practices.

Okay, I'll get off my rant about best practices and tell you when best practices make sense. If you come into a talent acquisition department that is completely broken, getting to best practices is probably a good first step to getting your feet on the ground and making some good things happen. If you're already pretty good, following best practices is the fastest way to stay mediocre.

6. **Experiment.** I'll discuss this concept in detail in the next chapter, but experimenting is truly the way to continually improve your processes within talent acquisition. It's a major weakness I see in many talent acquisition leaders at all levels in that we come into the role with our hair on fire wanting to change the world. Within a few months, or a few years, all of that has gone away. It's not that we changed the world; we just forgot about how it felt on that first day.

Amazon founder Jeff Bezos calls this "Day 1" leadership. Bezos introduced this concept in 1997 in a shareholder letter to all Amazon shareholders and employees, and I'm in love with the concept. Here is what it's all about in Bezos' own words:

> *I've been reminding people that it's Day 1 for a couple of decades. I work in an Amazon building named Day 1, and when I moved buildings, I took the name with me. I spend time thinking about this topic.*
>
> *Day 2 is stasis. Followed by irrelevance. Followed by excruciating, painful decline. Followed by death. And that is why it is always Day 1.*
>
> *To be sure, this kind of decline would happen in extreme slow motion. An established company may harvest Day 2 for decades, but the final result would still come.*
>
> *I'm interested in the question, how do you fend off Day 2? What are the techniques and tactics? How do you keep the vitality of Day 1, even inside a large organization?*
>
> *Such a question can't have a simple answer. There will be many elements, multiple paths and many traps. I don't know the whole answer, but I may know bits of it. Here's a starter pack of essentials for **Day 1 defense: customer obsession, a skeptical view of proxies, the eager adoption of external trends, and high-velocity decision-making.**[2]*

Day 1 talent acquisition leaders experiment and they don't stop experimenting, even when it's Day 2 because it never becomes Day 2. I believe we fend off Day 2 by constantly asking our teams and our organization to experiment.

7. **Expect excellence and reward high performance.** No one gets into the hall of fame for being average. Mediocrity is like cancer. If you don't address it quickly, it spreads and grows, and eventually, it kills your function and maybe even your organization. High performance starts with hiring, but it doesn't end there.

I constantly see corporate talent acquisition teams hiring high performing agency recruiters. I've even lost some of my own recruiters to corporate TA jobs. These are recruiters who were killing it in my environment and ninety days later they're pieces of garbage. Why? Because expectations were not set, and high performance was not rewarded.

What my former recruiters learned was that they could go into a corporate setting, do the same as everyone else, and the rewards and expectations just stayed the same. It's human nature, for most people, to do as little as possible to get the reward that is expected. It's up to the leader to set high expectations, and then significantly reward those who meet them and not reward those who do not.

The DNA of a Great Recruiter

For the past ten years I've been blogging about HR, talent acquisition, and leadership every single day at *Fistful of Talent* (FOT), and my own blog, *The Tim Sackett Project.*[3] (Named by *Fistful of Talent* founder, my good friend Kris Dunn, who says I'm contractually obligated to let people know he named my blog. There you go, KD!) The *Fistful of Talent* blog is a multi-contributor blog where at any one time ten to twelve or so writers are contributing smart, snarky content.

Over the years at FOT we've had some really great writers and talented HR and TA pros/leaders come through the ranks. One of the things we were able to pull from all of these folks was this notion that each of us was chosen because we had certain DNA that others did not. We had traits and abilities that obviously allowed us to write about HR and TA, but also we thought about HR and TA differently than our fellow HR and TA brothers and sisters.

This DNA was kind of a living idea that has grown and taken shape over the years, and I'm going to share with you what I believe the DNA of a great recruiter entails. When we first set out to look at this subject, it was more about our own DNA. What is about us that makes us different? That evolved into, What do we feel the DNA of any great HR professional may look like?

I've taken this one step further to ask the question, What does the DNA of great recruiter look like? What are those components? What is the mix needed? We think we know. Right now you're reading this and you have a mental picture in your head of the best recruiter you've ever worked with. You could list out all those things that made them great. Someone else is also reading this and they may have a different picture and traits. That is what makes this really hard.

So many different types of people can be successful in recruiting. It's not the gregarious, outgoing, can-talk-to-anyone person who is always successful in recruiting. Many times, it's the quiet, thoughtful person who is super successful in recruiting. So, personality type alone is not the answer.

Here are my eight components of a great recruiter's DNA:

1. **Connectivity.** Great recruiters love to recruit, and recruiting, at its foundation, is about being able to connect with others. It's one of the first things I look for when interviewing candidates for a recruiter position. I do not look for previous recruiting experience. I feel like recruiting is easily trained, if you hire the right person.

   That "right" person must be someone who easily connects with other people. Connection takes on a couple of different meanings in this component. First, I need individuals who are natural connectors of people. They are probably more active on social media sites, like Facebook, LinkedIn, Instagram, Snapchat, and X (formerly known as Twitter) than the average person. They also may be an in-person connector as well, involved with volunteer work, religion, sports teams, or clubs.

Every great recruiter I've worked with has some aspect of this type of connecting. It's easy for them to connect and go in and out of these situations with ease. They may be a part of a group, but haven't been in a while, and when going back they can instantly fall back in without too much work.

The other connection piece is being able to instantly connect with someone new. In recruiting we are constantly speaking and messaging with candidates every day we work. Most of these people we have never met, but our ability to recruit them comes down to our ability to quickly, almost instantly, build a connection. Great recruiters have this in their DNA.

There's a piece of this segment of your DNA that comes down to sheer likeability. Great recruiters have something in them that others like. I've never met a good recruiter who wasn't liked. It's hard to be effective in a role when everyone thinks you're an idiot. In fact, I've met a bunch of recruiters who were technically awesome at recruiting, but they rubbed most people the wrong way, and they failed. Don't ever underestimate the power of being liked when it comes to recruiting great talent.

Some people will call this charisma, but we all know when we meet someone for the first time if there's a good chance we'll like that person. As a leader, you will also see this in your first interview. No one wants to work with Eeyore; everyone likes Winnie.

2. **The ability to speak the truth.** You may say, "Well, everyone can speak the truth," and technically you would be right, but not everyone actually speaks the truth, so this becomes an important trait of great recruiters. What's even more valuable is the ability to speak the truth in a way that people will readily accept. If you can do that, now you're truly running with scissors.

In recruiting, we waste so much time because we are constantly playing this communication game with candidates. Dealing with real people, all day, who think they're the perfect fit for your job is hard. Great recruiters limit the amount of time they work for free.

"Working for free" is working with a candidate you'll never hire. The more time you give candidates you'll never hire, the more time you're working for free. Great recruiters master the ability to speak the truth in a way that is not offensive, but that ensures that candidate will understand exactly where they stand and not need more hand-holding.

This trait is also ultra-valuable when dealing with hiring managers, especially as the time we block out with hiring managers tends to be significant, and the biggest challenges to hiring quickly. Bad recruiters tend to not speak the truth when dealing with hiring managers; they tell the hiring manager what they want to hear, believing this leads to higher "customer satisfaction." Great recruiters tell the hiring manager the truth in a way that speeds along the process to a decision.

In an interview situation, I'll work to discover a candidate's ability to tell the truth by asking questions I know have only one truthful response, and the response is either tough to say or awkward in a normal interview environment. I'm a big Michigan State University (MSU) supporter and fan. If I was interviewing a candidate that I know is a University of Michigan (UofM) fan, I may ask him, "If you were to work here, we do a bunch of activities with MSU, would you be willing to wear MSU gear to work?" A real UofM fan would not say, "Yes." I want the truth. Are you willing to not get the job over something so trivial? Those with this DNA trait would figure out a way to say "no" but still maintain their desire for the job.

3. **Lack of a victim mentality.** The concept of "victim" mentality was first brought up as candidate DNA trait in the book *Journey to The Emerald City: Achieve a Competitive Edge by Creating a*

Culture of Accountability by Roger Connors and Tom Smith, who also wrote *The Oz Principle*.[4] Being a victim is placing blame on outside forces for things that happen.

"Well, I couldn't find you candidates for your position because we don't have a good ATS system." "It's not my fault the candidate didn't accept, we didn't offer enough money." "If we had a better website we could attract talent." "If you bought me a LinkedIn license I could find the candidates you need."

Have you heard any of these before? These are all victim statements. *Journey to the Emerald City* isn't a quick read, but once you read it you'll constantly catch yourself and others using victim statements, and you'll be able to recognize destructive victim behaviors. My wife and I will call each other out when we fall into the trap of being victims.

Great recruiters are not victims. Great recruiters find ways to make it happen regardless of the tools, resources, and time we're given. They do not let roadblocks stop them, or speed bumps slow them down. They rise above the victim mentality and make good things happen. Recruiters face constant rejection, so having the DNA trait of not being a victim is critical to success.

When looking at candidates, it's fairly easy to pull out or discover victim behaviors. If you ask about a team project that failed, a victim will quickly place blame on team members while telling you how they tried to make it succeed. A true anti-victim behavior would be to take responsibility and explain what they did to remedy the situation.

4. **Marketing chops.** Marketing skills have increasingly become a valuable skill for great recruiting. Of course, a potential recruiter can pick up formal marketing chops through education and experience, but it can also be as simple as having a natural ability to just be savvier when it comes to being able to market or sell a product or service.

Those who do fraternity and sorority recruitment are great natural marketers.. It doesn't have to be complex. Can you talk a freshman student into selecting your sorority over the one across the street? It's shocking how many of us can't.

The classic interview example is to give the candidate your pen and ask her to sell you the pen back. But this is another trait you'll see come up in examples throughout your questioning of potential recruiters. Taking a look at your current career site, what changes would they recommend making to entice others into applying? A natural marketer will have many ideas that they can come up with quickly.

Candidates with marketing chops also think about talent acquisition differently than someone who grew up in the HR world. You'll see it when they look at processes. They focus on the candidate first; not how the process helps TA, but how the process can work better for the candidate. That's a marketing approach, not an HR approach.

5. **The ability to close.** Great recruiters close. They rarely have a candidate get to the final stages and turn down the offer. The ability to close is critical to recruiting success. Most talent acquisition leaders will develop training sessions just on closing and run them several times per year.

   "A.B.C.—Always Be Closing" is a classic sales line. Salespeople are trained from day one how to close a customer. Recruiters are no different. Your ability to close as a recruiter will make or break your career.

   Great recruiting closers share one natural trait and I call it the "jealous spouse" (to be fair, it works with whether you're a girlfriend or a boyfriend, but I've only experienced it from a girlfriend). A jealous spouse will question her boyfriend about any little thing that doesn't seem right if she feels something is wrong about a situation. "So, you left the bar at 11 p.m., but it's now 11:45 p.m. and the bar is only 20 minutes away?" "Oh, you stopped for gas. What station?" "Didn't you just get gas two days ago?"

   The best recruiters I've ever worked with, male or female, were great jealous spouses. They don't have a filter when it comes to asking every single question that doesn't line up just perfectly because they know a hiring manager will see it and ask. The last thing great recruiters want to happen is a question being asked that they don't know the answer to.

Also, asking all these questions is how you properly close a candidate. Offers fall apart at the end because questions were left unasked at the beginning. "So, you're interested in our company and job, but this seems like it would add twenty minutes on to your drive. Have you made this drive yet at rush hour? What will adding forty minutes on to your day do to your personal schedule at home?" "So, you're making $65,000 a year in your current role. Our position pays $70,000 max. If we offer the job at $70,000 what will keep you from accepting? Benefits cost? Paid time off? 401(k) match? Is there anything that could stop this?" Always be closing.

6. **Consultative skills.** The best recruiters become talent consultants to hiring managers. It's not about doing the job of a recruiter for them; it's about delivering expertise. I'm the expert in the organization on talent, and I'm here to advise you on the best course of action you need to take that will put you and your department in the best situation, even if that means more work for me. So, it's not about just filling requisitions and helping myself out.

Consultative skills allow a recruiter to become a valued member of the hiring manager's inner circle, someone they rely on when making hiring decisions. But many times, it leads to making any kind of personnel decision within their department. Consultants deliver advice based on their knowledge and expertise, and great recruiters have this DNA trait.

When I interview recruiters, I'll have candidates advise me on things we could do to better help them as candidates. It's something they know well. They know how they want to be treated. Advise me, be a consultant to our candidate experience. Help me understand what I don't know about how this experience affected you. Someone with consultative skills can easily do this.

The recruiters who can put themselves into the role of consultant also have the ability to understand the importance of building trusting relationships. Consultants work for the client. That's who is (theoretically) paying them. So, consultants will first work on building and gaining trust. No hiring manager ever took advice from someone they didn't trust had their best interest in mind.

7. **Being a futurist.** Having futurist DNA is about your ability to continue to look forward in the industry and market to not only see what may be next but also having the desire to know what may be next. I want recruiters working for me who are constantly looking within our industry and market trends—not just trends within talent acquisition. As a leader, I'll be doing that in the functions they are supporting to help stay ahead of our competition.

   If I'm recruiting nurses, I better know the direction of this industry if I want to stay in front of it from a recruiting perspective. When I was working in the health system in Michigan, there was a strategy shift from hiring both LPNs and RNs to only hiring RNs. As a recruiting team, we went and worked with RN programs around the state to ensure we had a pipeline of candidates two years before this went into effect.

   When I was in the retail industry, I would meet with our real estate and construction leadership teams to know where they were looking at new potential builds so I could keep on top of recruiting pools in those areas, sometimes as far out as two years. When you open a new location, you have a short time to hire and train a full team. If I could build a pipeline of talent a year or two prior, that made the job that much easier to accomplish.

   I want to be surrounded by recruiters who are constantly asking me for tools I've never heard of. It doesn't mean that I'm going to go out and buy all of this stuff, but I know they're constantly looking for the latest and greatest. If a recruiter never comes to me and asks about some new tool in the marketplace, I seriously question whether they care about their skill development.

8. **Fearlessness.** I wanted to title this DNA trait "the ability to pick up the f****** phone," but I thought that may offend someone.

I've gotten to the point now when interviewing new recruiter candidates that I'll have them call and interview me as the first step of the process. As you can imagine, some folks really struggle with this. More often than not, those who struggle would make crappy recruiters.

Recruiters have to talk to candidates. Talking to candidates means you must pick up a phone and dial it. It's amazing how many people get hired into recruiting roles who are scared to pick up a phone and call and talk to someone. We go through an entire interview process and we don't even know if they can do the one skill they will have to do every day.

Then, as leaders, we are shocked to find out that Billy doesn't like to pick up the phone and he's an awful recruiter. My first three weeks on the job as an entry-level recruiter, I only made phone calls. From a stack of résumés, I was required to make one hundred calls per day before I could go home.

After three weeks, and after connecting with hundreds of people, I took the stack into my boss's office. He looked at me, took the résumés, then turned around and threw them into his trash can. He handed me a job requisition and said, "Okay, now you're ready. Go fill this job."

The entire exercise for three weeks was to break my fear of picking up the phone and calling people. Every talent acquisition leader I know underestimates the importance of this. This is why recruiter candidates now interview me, as a first step. We aren't launching the space shuttle; we are just talking to people on the phone. If you can't talk to me on the phone, you can't work for me as a recruiter.

There is a direct correlation between the number of phone calls a recruiter makes and their success, in both corporate talent acquisition and agency. Direct correlation. More calls equal more jobs filled. Every industry. Every market. Don't allow your recruiters to tell you differently. They're lying to you. They're afraid to pick up the freaking phone.

Here's the thing . . .

Surround yourself with a team that is bought into your vision of the future. Fire everyone else. Every single day, Talent Acquisition leaders are fired because they tried converting recruiters who didn't want to be converted, and it ultimately took them down. This is a waste of time. Set your vision. Discover those who are bought into that vision. Move forward with them.

» 7 «

The Recruiter's Superpower

Every recruiter has a superpower. It's the exact same superpower for every recruiter. It's also the exact same superpower that every single other person has, but few actually truly master how to use it. Recruiters use this superpower more than any other profession besides sex workers.

That superpower is our ability to make someone feel wanted.

It's a universal psychological emotion that every single person on the planet is addicted to. We all want to be wanted by someone or something. As recruiters, we are in a unique position to use this superpower every single day.

Right now, your phone is ringing. You have a great job. Great pay. Great flexibility. There is really no reason for you to want to leave your job. Things are going very well for you. But when you pick up that phone it's me. I want to talk to you about "an opportunity" I have available that I think you would be perfect for. (Author's Note: By the way—I would never tell you I have an opportunity for you! That sounds weird.) Most people will thank me and hang up. They aren't interested, it was the wrong title, wrong location, wrong pay, and so on. We all know the game.

It's the next thing you do that is telling on how powerful our recruiting superpower is! As soon as you hang up with me, turning my job down, you start looking for someone to tell. "Hey, I just got this silly call, they were recruiting me. Of course, I said beat it! I love my job. I mean, really, trying to recruit me."

We can't wait to tell someone else! I was wanted! You weren't! I was!

As recruiters, there will come a time when you have to try and recruit a certain subset of candidates who at the time are being overly recruited. We've seen this for years in information technology (IT). You call an IT professional and they lose their minds. "Stop calling me!" Then they're with their family at Sunday dinner and that's all they talk about. "Ugh! I mean it's awful, I get ten calls a day. I can't stand it!" Do you know what they really can't stand? Not being called at all!

It's the one piece of advice I love giving to new recruiters. The thing that will get them through the tough times when it feels like no one wants the job they are working on. You have this one unbelievably powerful superpower and don't ever forget it. Remember it on your darkest day. You get to make people feel wanted. And while they might act like they don't want to be wanted, remember what they'll do the moment they hang up with you. They're going to tell someone that is close to them they are desired!

I get asked a lot by organizations to help them get better at recruiting. Many of these organizations will come to me and tell me that they have nothing going for them. They trail the market in compensation. Their brand is garbage. Their managers aren't any good. They believe they have no worthy attributes to sell to candidates.

I will tell them you still have one thing left you can do. You can make your potential candidates feel like you want them more than your competition. In fact, your competition for talent is probably cocky and is making too many candidates feel like they are unwanted. While it's still going to be hard, you will be able to hire some good people by just showing them you want them more than anyone else does.

I've gotten asked a million times what I like about recruiting. For the longest time, I told people I was attracted to the emotion of helping someone find that job. Their first job. A better job. A job after being out of work for a long period. Their dream job. But in reality, I was addicted to how I can make someone else feel. It's an amazing feeling to make others feel good about themselves. It's a weird type of power you have over all of these random people that you've never met. They don't even know it's happening to them until it's over.

Those who hate recruiting focus on the rejection side of recruitment. You will talk to so many candidates who will tell you "no." That is true. But the vast majority of the "nos" also came with the feeling that you made them feel better about themselves. For a little while in their day, they had the confidence of knowing they were wanted by someone.

Great recruiters are masterful in making you feel wanted. Making you feel desired. It's the superpower each of us has in recruiting and we have an endless supply of it.

Here's the thing . . .

It's basic human psychology that we all want to be desired by someone else. It's been this way since the beginning of time. There is no greater power you have at your disposal in recruiting than this.

Building the High-Volume Hiring Machine Your Competition Doesn't Have!

"It ought to be remembered that there is nothing more difficult to take in hand, more perilous to conduct, or more uncertain in its success, than to take the lead in the introduction of a new order of things. Because the innovator has for enemies all those who have done well under the old conditions, and luke-warm defenders in those who may do well under the new. This coolness arises partly from fear of the opponents, who have the laws on their side, and partly from the incredulity of men, who do not readily believe in new things until they have had a long experience of them."

—Niccolò Machiavelli, *The Prince*

Warning

This chapter will make you enemies. It will make you enemies because people hate change, even when they tell you they don't. This chapter is going to teach how to build an innovative and award-winning hiring machine. To implement a new order of things in a big organization requires great change, something you'll be hated for. You've been warned.

Recruiting is hard. Recruiting is exponentially easier if you can build the perfect hiring machine for your organization. Building a great hiring machine isn't just about technology. If it were, most of us would already have a great hiring machine working for us. But most of us don't.

A machine takes many parts working together in exact precision to run correctly. The machine needs fuel and lubrication. The machine needs routine maintenance and upkeep. Your talent acquisition department, in many aspects, is a machine. You have all the parts—your people, processes, and technology. The trick is understanding how to build this machine, get it up and running, and maintain it at a highly consistent level. This is where most talent acquisition (TA) leaders fail.

Every machine built in history had a purpose. Our hiring machine also has a straightforward purpose. We need to hire more employees. The issue is that each machine we build for this purpose will differ because we all face different conditions. In the North, we build snow removal machines because we tend to get snow. People in the South don't need snow removal machines. A snowblower in Florida is worthless. Each hiring machine, while having the same purpose, can actually be very different. If you are trying to hire ten thousand low-skill workers, your machine will have certain characteristics that someone trying to hire twenty certified public accountants won't have, and vice versa.

This has been one of the major failure points in talent acquisition for decades. We built an applicant tracking system (ATS) that was to act like our all-in-one hiring machine. The problem is that hiring a low-skill, no-skill worker for a part-time or seasonal job is drastically different than hiring a software engineer. We were using one machine to do two very different jobs.

I've broken down the build of our TA machine into ten segments that you'll have to pay attention to. Those segments are:

1. Being the Right Leader
2. Is the Organization Feeling Enough Pain?
3. It Takes the Right Design to Work
4. The Right Technology
5. Get Your Hiring Managers on Board

6. Get Your Politics Under Control
7. Your Machine Must Be Metrics-Driven
8. The Right Job Advertising
9. Find the Money
10. You're Going to Be on an Island

Let's dig into each segment so you have some understanding of what you're going to run into as you build your hiring machine.

1—Being the Right Leader

I've met very high-level talent acquisition leaders at some of the largest companies in the world. After interacting with these people, I thought to myself, "That person is an idiot!" Now, "idiot" is probably too strong of an adjective. They didn't seem to have the skills I would expect for such a big job. Then it occurred to me. If you run talent acquisition at Google or Apple, you don't really have to be that talented. (Author's note: I'm not talking about the TA leaders who currently work at Google and Apple, I'm sure they are wonderful, pretty people.) That's because those brands are unicorn brands. Unicorn brands don't really have to attract talent. Talent finds them. What you have to be is a masterful project manager and most likely elite at dealing with organizational politics. But, honestly, you don't really need many talent acquisition skills to be successful.

Now, you might work at a big name unicorn brand that is broken for some reason, and that will take a masterful recruiting leader to turn the ship around. I also know many of these leaders, and I'm lucky to call some my friends. Many have contributed to this book!

In the talent acquisition industry, we see companies turn over TA leaders at a frequency we do not see in other functions. Why? It's because these organizations are hiring a talent acquisition leader, but they most likely aren't hiring the "right" talent acquisition leader for their current situation.

Let me give you a quick example. I often see mid-enterprise companies that have broken hiring functions go out and hire a new TA leader who is coming from a well-running unicorn brand. Think Midwest manufacturing company or health system hiring a talent acquisition director from Google. What does this Google talent leader know about broken recruiting functions? Nothing. They worked in a perfect talent lab their entire career. They've had massive recruiting budgets and access to the most innovative and latest recruiting technology. They have no idea about how to turn around a broken shop. They most likely are not the "right" leader for this situation, but boy, does their résumé look great!

It's not just a selection issue. It's also a self-insight issue. The TA leader taking these jobs must know if they can actually do this or not. Too often, we have TA leaders taking on roles they know they can't do, and it's probably going to hurt their career, but they're getting 20 percent more and a nicer title. I don't blame them for wanting to advance, but it's a recipe for failure almost always.

In building an excellent hiring machine, you must first have the right leader to help you build that machine. I work with dozens of enterprise organizations by coming in and analyzing their talent acquisition function. Over 50 percent of the time, I find that these organizations have some leadership execution issues that will hinder their success. Usually, the chief human resources officer (CHRO) or Head of Talent is good, but they've promoted leaders up through the organization that lack the skills to make a transformation happen. However, they also feel loyalty to these people, and reskilling high-level leadership behaviors is almost impossible, especially when you're trying to turn some around from where it's been. You might be the right leader, but you're surrounded by a team that is incapable of helping you build your machine.

2—Is the Organization Feeling Enough Pain?

Big change doesn't happen when everyone is fat and happy. One of the critical elements to building or rebuilding your hiring machine in the way you need it is pain. Unfortunately, it's a key ingredient.

In reality, many organizations have this pain, and we keep throwing Advil and Band-Aids at it, hoping that will cure our cancer. I think it was one of the most masterful leadership gurus of our time, Taylor Swift, who said, "Band-Aids don't fix bullet holes." Like always, Taylor is correct. The recognition that your pain is terminal is the next step on your build journey. This recognition can't just be by you. It has to be at the highest levels of your organization. Your CEO must recognize this pain. Having them on board will be key to your success.

In private conversations with CHROs and talent leaders, I will make the statement that if we could just cut out everyone else in the organization and sit down with the CEO, we could solve almost every recruiting problem we have in an hour. I truly believe this because when I get the opportunity to have this conversation with the CEO, they 100 percent are bought in and ready to make the change. They will be your biggest champion to get this right. Why? Because every single CEO in history will tell anyone who wants to listen that "talent is our most important asset."

I know this sounds counterintuitive. If we did leadership in a lab environment, we would say that we should be able to do great change without pain. In fact, ideally, the best change shouldn't have pain. We should just see something that needs to be changed and be able to do it. Unfortunately, we don't work in a laboratory vacuum. We live in real life. In our real world, we have to worry about things like profit, expenses, margin, and so on. Thus, change happens only when it absolutely is the last option we have to make something better.

3—It Takes the Right Design to Work!

Okay, we've got the right leader, and we have pain motivation. Now what the heck are we going to do? This is where experience in building and hiring machines is critical. There are a couple of ways to get this experience that I've seen work effectively. One is you get thrown into the deep end of the pool as a leader, and you survive! You get a chance to build a machine. You probably aren't ready, but you get lucky, and you pull it off. Now you know a few things, and you have confidence in a design that will work.

Trial and error, though, is not the only way to get the right design for your machine. Turns out, a lot of vendors are critical parts to these machines and they've actually built some successful machines for clients. Stealing a design and tweaking it to be your own is another great way to build a pretty good first version of your hiring machine, and it might be the fastest way to build it. I'll talk about the technology in the next segment, but this is less about the technology and more about how the technology designs the full machine. You can often find other talent acquisition leaders who have built really good machines, find out whom they use from a technology perspective, and the vendor will give you the design, hoping you'll use them on the technology side to build your machine. I see this in industries all the time. Big hospital healthcare is a classic example. Once one health system builds the machine, it can almost be copied exactly for another. It is ironic that healthcare tends to lag in talent acquisition when there are some amazing machines that have been built in the space. Higher education is another industry that lags but doesn't have to.

One part of the machine design that failed for decades was TA shops building a machine that worked for them, not for the candidate. We are living in a world where candidates will hold the power in the hiring process, and it's going to get worse. You must build a hiring machine that is candidate-first. Every part of your design must be looked at through that lens. It's not about making your job in TA easier. That's an old TA design. It's about making it so simple that a candidate can show interest in seconds. Most organizations still have a hiring machine that requires candidates to survive the process.

4—The Right Technology

Never build your hiring machine on technology that is unproven at the size and scope you're at, especially if your organization is conservative in nature. The classic leadership saying was always, "You'll never get fired for using IBM." There is some truth to that at enterprise-level organizations. If you're an SMB or even smaller mid-enterprise, you can take some chances on unproven technology that has a ton of upside. The cost will be lower, and if it fails, you're probably back to where you started with some great learning, and it didn't cost you much. You can't do that when you're in a big company. There's too much risk.

This doesn't mean, though, that you build a hiring machine that has already been shown not to get the results you need. You still have to reach for some next-gen technology. I just caution you to try it yourself first. Or, if possible, test it on a smaller segment of your organization to validate and then roll it out to the wider organization accordingly.

One of the biggest advancements in talent acquisition technology in recent years has been the use of conversational artificial intelligence (AI) and its ability to help organizations convert more interested potential candidates into actual applicants. The leader in this technology is Paradox. There are other technology vendors in this space as well, including Humanly, Harri, Workstream, and Fountain.

How is this high-volume hiring technology different from your typical Applicant Tracking System (ATS) or Human Capital Management (HCM) Recruiting module? Primarily, most ATSs are built for professional, white-collar hiring. Candidates who are willing to sit in front of a laptop and take fifteen to twenty-five minutes to jump through your application hoops. Systems like Paradox are designed specifically with the hourly worker in mind. Someone who will most likely have to apply using a mobile device and probably won't take longer than five minutes to apply, if that.

These high-volume hiring technologies are designed to be used by managers who do hiring as part of their job and probably don't have a full-time recruiter working with them on their normal daily and weekly hiring needs. So, someone like a general manager of a restaurant, hotel, or retail location. These types of hiring managers need something easy, light, fast, and most likely mobile. Hiring new employees is one of a hundred things they have on their priority list each week.

This isn't to say that a traditional ATS can't help you hire hourly workers. They can and have been doing this task for decades. But high-volume hiring technology built on conversational AI is simply a better-built mousetrap for this hiring purpose.

I wanted to give you some insight from the man who had a hand in creating this space—Aaron Matos, the founder and CEO of Paradox. Aaron is one of those people in recruiting technology that just "gets it" at a very high level. I interviewed Aaron about the difficulty of making the right recruiting technology choices for your organization:

Why do most TA departments, at the enterprise level, struggle to pick the right technology to solve their hiring problem?

(Aaron Matos)—There are a few big issues.

First, there are so many dynamics at play in large, global companies—internal politics, bureaucracy, influence from the IT organization, and, often, requirements to go to RFP from procurement (which sometimes leads to the most economical decision, not necessarily the right one). These dynamics promote the status quo because they often resist or stand in the way of real change and transformation.

Second, status quo. See above. Change is hard—especially when it means betting your job or your reputation on it. Unfortunately, when fear dictates decisions, we tend to see a regression to the mean. Put another way: Everyone takes the predictable path because it's "safe" instead of the one that might help you solve a problem in a more meaningful, differentiated way.

Third, companies sometimes take a one-size-fits-all approach to hiring—buying technology that generally serves the entire organization and all hiring needs instead of technologies that have been purpose-built to solve specific hiring challenges. The problem with that is obvious: Not all candidates are the same—especially when it comes to corporate and hourly jobs. How you design the hiring process for a frontline warehouse job should be entirely different than how you design it for a corporate data scientist role. Yet, most companies buy technology that effectively treats those candidates exactly the same.

When you think about building a high-volume hiring machine, where will most organizations fail? What's going to wrong that we can stop them or fix it before it goes bad?

(Matos)—They'll fail by not doing enough—or by doing too much. I know, I know. That's a paradox. :)

I always encourage clients to ask themselves: "What would you do if anything was possible?" High-volume hiring is all about speed and simplicity. The company that responds to a candidate first—and gets them through the process the fastest—is the company that usually hires them. You have to evaluate your process and technology through that lens. What would you do if you were given the keys to completely redesign your process? What would it look like?

Spend time understanding the real pain in your process—and mapping out a plan to remove as much of it as humanly possible without creating unnecessary change. Talk to people who've actually applied to your jobs. Talk to your frontline managers and recruiters. What would they want your process to look like if they were given the keys? Map out every single minute of your hiring process and identify anything that's creating unnecessary friction or waiting. Make things easy. And when you roll out this change internally, make it crystal clear why your new process will make your managers and recruiter's jobs better.

Matos also shared, which I agree with 100 percent, that ultimately, your candidates, recruiters, and managers don't care what technology you buy—or why you bought it. They care that whatever you buy can help them—either by making something easier or faster or by getting the boring stuff done for them, so they can spend time on the people stuff that technology can't or shouldn't do. People aren't dreading automation. They now expect it. And often, when they get to experience it, they overwhelmingly say "thank you."

5—Get Your Hiring Managers on Board

Seems like this is pretty obvious, but it's another huge failure point for most organizations. I find the best way to do this is to not get all of your hiring managers on board. Start with one or a few, test your design, refine it, and get it working really well. I can't say this enough. HR and TA have failed so many times in big project rollouts because we want to do the entire organization all at once, and that strategy almost always fails.

You actually have a broken process running right now. Let it continue. For many, it's comfortable and common, and they don't really know it's broken. Let them continue to live in this dream state. You have some hiring managers that are in severe pain. Start with those poor souls first. They'll love the attention and the effort you are giving to try and help them. They'll be more involved. They will become your internal champions of change when you get it working the way it should be.

For the most part, 90 percent of your hiring managers will eventually get on board, and they'll have no issues with your new hiring machine. We will always have some outliers. Some problem children. This is common for all organizations. I would love to tell you just to fire them. Oh, can you imagine if it was just that easy? Praised be!

You don't need to get every hiring manager on board. If you build the right machine that works well, the vast majority of hiring managers will be on board. You'll then have to "influence" the others to comply. My favorite way to "influence" laggard hiring managers is to call a meeting with them, yourself, and someone much higher up. Their boss. Your boss. The CEO if you can get them to show up. Immediately, the hiring manager will message you to find out what this meeting is about. I want you to simply respond with, "Your unwillingness to follow our hiring process." Don't give anything extra. Keep it short and simple. If you do this, 99 percent of the time that meeting will never happen because the hiring manager will cave at the thought of having to explain why they're being an asshole. If it does happen, rejoice in the fact you have built something great, with great results, and for some reason, this person doesn't want to be a team player.

6—Get Your Politics Under Control

We tend to think "politics" is everything outside of our own function. "Ugh! The chief information officer (CIO) is causing problems and wants to do their own thing because technology is so special!" Yes, this does happen, but the politics that will cause you the most problem are the politics you'll face from your own internal team.

You see, we all become creatures of habit. Making a giant change in your organization causes even bigger changes to your own team and other functions within HR more broadly. You might be trying to build a better hiring machine, but that new machine can also impact payroll, onboarding, HR technology, talent management, and so on. Each of these functions might be thinking, and it might even be true, that their function has never run better. Why should we change anything?

You get your politics under control by getting all stakeholders and your vision champion (usually the CEO or high-level C-suite executive feeling the most pain) on the same page. This takes more than an email telling everyone to get on board. You need to hear grievances and potential problems and roadblocks. You need to invite some highly influential partners to your project. You must overcommunicate constantly. You need this talked about, in a positive way, by the employees in your company that others listen to and trust.

Many great machines fail before being built because this step is missed or under-resourced.

7—Your Machine Must be Metrics-Driven

When I say "metrics-driven," I'm not saying that your machine should have the ability to collect important metrics of your talent acquisition function. Any ATS can collect important metrics of your talent acquisition function. I mean, you should build a machine around the metrics you want to measure. You should understand which metrics measure true success in your organization, and build a machine that will capture what you need throughout the process. If I talk to one hundred TA leaders, they will all tell me they are collecting TA metrics. Less than 10 percent of those TA leaders will be able to define how they measure success with those metrics. Don't just collect data to collect data. Collect the data that proves your success in TA.

I will tell you that I prefer you have live metrics. At any point in time, you should be able to get into your machine and give me a snapshot of exactly where you're at today. Not last month. Not last week. Today. You get bonus points if you can tell me in real time. That's hard to do, but some will get there.

If you're going to build a hiring machine, you need to be able to show your organization whether it's working or not. This means you need funnel metrics by the individual recruiter, by location, by function, by department, and so on. You need to be able to show your executive team what your capacity for recruiting is in the organization. You. Do. Not. Need. To. Show. How. Long. It. Took. To. Fill. A. Position. That metric is basically worthless. Time to fill is not a TA success metric. It's a TA health metric. There is zero correlation between your team recruiting faster and you being better at recruiting. Please read that last line again. If the industry average to fill a position is 37 days, and you're at 36.2 days, you aren't better. Also, if you're at 38.3 days, you're not worse. You're in the ballpark, and that's fine. If your time to fill is 87 days? You've got cancer and need desperate help.

Stop measuring stuff that has zero correlation to recruiting success just because you have the data.

There is a direct correlation between better recruiting and the number of candidates you screen and send to a hiring manager to interview. There is a direct correlation between better recruiting and the number of interviews that take place, to the number of offers that get accepted. If you can specifically tell your executive team that we are at 90 percent of our recruiting capacity and we can give you twenty more hires next quarter, that's real business data they can use. You need to be able to prove, without a shadow of a doubt, that your machine is working. That means hard data, not subjective, easily manipulated data. Below-average TA leaders do that. Be better.

8—The Right Job Advertising

When it comes to building our hiring machine, you will either have good organic candidate flow ("organic" meaning candidates coming to you without you having to pay for them), or you'll have to buy that candidate flow. The best candidates are free candidates, but most brands don't get enough free candidates, and you'll be forced to spend some money on job advertising to fill the top of your recruiting funnel.

Advertising works. Job advertising also works. My best friend, Kris Dunn, says I'm a slave to the Instagram advertising algorithm, and he's right. If there is some kind of new golf polo brand or athletic wear, it's going to find me, and I'm most likely buying it at least once. We are all suckers for great advertising. Within the recruiting industry, most job advertising is done via employment brand agencies or directly by using programmatic job advertising technology. By the way, if you're using an agency, they are using the same programmatic technology that you could use yourself. They are just white-labeling an off-the-shelf programmatic engine to buy your job ads and then up charging you.

While this is technology, this is different from your core hiring machine technology. Some more modern ATSs have actually built in some programmatic features, and I suspect that over time more and more will join in. This usually shows up as a feature like a "boost" button you can push when you need more candidates for a certain job or location. Hit the button, the programmatic technology goes to work, and somewhere along the way, you get an invoice.

You have three major costs in your hiring machine: labor, technology, and advertising. One critical item you need to know is whether or not your job advertising is working and where it is working best. Your advertising data might be some of the more important data to measure for success. Traditionally, average TA shops would mostly ignore what was happening on Indeed, LinkedIn, ZipRecruiter, and so on. It was just a cost of doing business. Today's TA leader must be aware of what is being spent, where it is being spent, and how we can incrementally spend those dollars better.

9—Find the Money

Real money. Not HR money! What's "HR money"? HR money is when a vendor tells you using their technology will reduce your cost by X percent because it reduces turnover or increases retention, and by saving all those employees, you'll save the company $47 million dollars in year one. No, you won't. That's never happened in the history of HR technology. That return on investment is built on made-up numbers that no CFO or CEO believes. You need to find real money that is being spent or will be spent and not have it be spent on the actual budget line.

That can sound like I'm asking you to do more with less. When in fact, many times when you're building your hiring machine, you need to spend more money. Both of these facts can be true at the same time. Of course, if you are overspending in some aspect of TA and your new machine allows you overall spend less, well, that's an easy sell. The larger the company, the more recruiting waste you'll find. That waste is usually found in third-party spending (recruitment process outsourcing, agency, temporary, contingent, etc.). Most large companies don't view this as recruiting spend because it's invoiced back directly to the business or department. Since it's not in TA's budget, you can claim the savings.

Our reality is that a great portion of third-party spending is because our hiring machine is failing. It takes one conversation with a CFO or director of finance to be able to connect the dots and for you to be able to claim these savings. So, you might need one million to build your hiring machine, but it's going to directly reduce RPO spend by three million. Thus, you have real money savings of two million dollars. Every finance department will sign up for this. All you have to do is care enough to dig into the money that is being spent because TA is failing. Therein lies our biggest struggle. Once we uncover the truth, we can longer hide from it.

In my experience, I've found that finding the money to build your hiring machine is the easiest part of building your machine, but most TA and HR leaders believe it's the hardest thing. The hardest thing is admitting to finance and the executive team that TA is failing, and I can show you exactly how much it's failing in dollars. For my third-party friends reading this, this does not mean that you only have jobs if TA fails. Of course, for decades, you've taken advantage of this failure, but the real "partnership" happens when you are filling capacity voids, not leveraging your "partner's" TA failure.

10—You're Going to Be on an Island!

I wanted to title this segment "No One F@cking Cares, But You!" That will be the reality of most TA Leaders that take on this endeavor. It's the dirty little secret no one wants to tell you. You're probably telling yourself that this fact doesn't matter. You can do it! Rah-Rah!

You're wrong. It will matter more than you think. It matters because when things get hard, you'll be all by yourself fighting this battle. And for what? No one is going to give you a trophy. You most likely won't be recognized for making something work properly that should have always worked properly. Building a great hiring machine is a labor of love, not recognition and accolades.

I can say those who build really good machines will never be out of a job. So, there's definitely a bump from a career standpoint because once you know how to do it, there's an endless list of companies that need it done. Career security is all but assured.

What could go wrong?

I mean, besides, you totally bombing this and losing your job and bankrupting the company?!

Here are the biggest hurdles you're going to face:

- You won't find enough money to do this right because the money you need is hitting non-HR budgets, and you simply don't have the juice in your organization to track it down and consolidate it. This is why I'm telling you to make friends with finance!
- Your spend to build the machine and what it is currently costing your organization to hire just doesn't add up. This is why it's critical to have enough pain. If things are working "okay," and you try and spend a bunch of money to do this, you will not have support.
- You personally don't have the skills to execute this, nor do you have the skills on your team to prop you up to get it done. Know your limitations. This isn't an entry-level leadership task.
- You aren't data-driven. You believe you are, but honestly, just between us, you aren't. This only makes sense in a data-driven world.
- You aren't close enough to the technology build, and the vendors are going to take advantage of you on delivery and cost.
- You don't do the roadshow and tell everyone the good news and early wins, which allows all of your detractors to talk sh*t about you and create doubt.

I believe it's important for you to go into everything as a leader with your eyes wide open. While I know this is the right course of action for every organization, ultimately, not every organization will be ready to do this at the same time. Many will grow into this understanding of what is needed, and it might take years for you to get your organization to this spot.

If it's going to take you some time, do the little things that will lead your organization down the path. Create a culture in which talent acquisition in going to be innovative and try things. Start small, but be relentless in your testing and experimentation. Over-communicate your testing when it's successful and when it fails.

Finally, be ready for the conversation. At some point, you will be confronted by an executive with a question like, "Hey, how do we fix this?" It might be in the elevator passing by or during a board meeting, but it's going to come. You have three minutes to convince them to build the hiring machine. It won't take much convincing because they are desperate for you to do this, but you must sound confident like you already know how to pull this off. Thankfully, you now do!

Here's the thing . . .

If you build the machine once, you'll be able to build it again anywhere else. Building the machine might be the hardest thing you'll do in your TA career, but it will give you the best career insurance of all time. Executing this is very difficult, which is why so few have done it.

» 9 «

The TA Tech Stack for the Rest of Us

The world of talent acquisition technology has never been in a more confusing and overwhelming place. William Tincup, president at RecruitingDaily and overall human resources (HR) and talent acquisition (TA) genius, estimates that there are more than 20,000 different HR and TA technology products on the planet, and the segment is growing at a feverish pace.[1] It's not surprising that most TA leaders have no idea where to start and where to go.

I will say when it comes to technology and hiring, technology is not needed to hire.

Yeah, I said it. I'm a huge fan of the technology space in HR and TA, but we can hire employees with zero technology. Why do I make this statement? Because too many in our industry become victims to their technology stack.

"We can't hire because our ATS is awful." "If I just had a LinkedIn Recruiter seat, I could find the talent you need." "We need to post our jobs on more sites if we want to compete." "If we only had that new artificial intelligence sourcing tool, we wouldn't have any problems hiring the employees we need."

That's all garbage for the most part.

If you suck at recruiting, the only thing technology will do is make you suck faster.

Technology doesn't make a TA shop great. You first have to be able to do the basic blocking and tackling of recruiting. Too often, I go into a TA shop with a new leader and the first thing they want to focus on is changing the technology.

Usually, this happens because the team the new leader inherited is saying this is the real problem. It's not. The real problem is that no real recruiting is taking place, but blaming technology is a great way to get the pressure off someone who doesn't really know how to recruit effectively.

Your TA tech stack can make a good TA shop great. It can also make a weak TA shop disastrous. More times than not, I see HR and TA technology implementations struggle to live up to expectations, or completely fail, and it has absolutely nothing to do with the technology and everything to do with who is using that technology.

So, before you go changing your technology for the sake of changing technology, you need do a few things.

Help Your Recruiters Become Great Recruiters

As TA leaders, we've done a pretty poor job at training recruiters to recruit. We rely on our technology vendors to show our recruiters some basic things, and then sit back and wonder why this huge investment we made isn't delivering the return on investment (ROI) we were promised. Before you make your next technology investment, invest in training your team to recruit. Find some professionals that can come in and really train your recruiters in the skills of sourcing, screening, and closing a candidate.

Work as a team to get better at delivering a world-class talent advisor consulting experience to your hiring managers. I promise you, if your team is fully trained and using their training, you could turn off your technology completely, and your organization wouldn't even notice. Great recruiters recruit, whether they have the technology or not.

Stop Breaking Your TA Technology

The HR and TA vendors reading this will probably highlight this section and send it to those customers who are struggling with the technology they've purchased. In TA, we are constantly asking the technology vendors we work with to break their technology for us.

When a piece of TA technology is developed, it's developed under one best-in-class way of doing whatever the problem is it's being developed to solve. In other words, this technology company has figured out a way to solve a problem. They built it as a process. And when used as it's designed, it works extremely well at solving that problem.

Along comes a client who has thousands of dollars to spend that the TA technology company desperately wants, and the client (you and I) ask the technology company to "change" or "configure" the technology to fit our process, not the process of the tech company. The tech company representatives, who need money to survive, comply, even though they know it will mess up their technology and make it not work as well.

We (the buyers of TA technology) break the technology we want to solve our problems by making the technology companies try to fit their technology into our broken processes. "Hey, we really suck at hiring, but we want to buy your technology to help us, but first, break your technology to fit our broken processes, because we are in control and are paying you money, and we have no idea what we are doing."

Sound a little bit familiar, at all?

Every TA leader and TA department needs to stop doing this. Throw away your broken processes that aren't giving you the results you need. Adopt the processes of the technology you are buying, which these vendors spent millions of dollars on and had experts develop to address your specific problem, and try something new and better.

It will work. No, it really will! These companies are in business to make stuff work, not make it not work. Stop asking them to make their technology not work.

Have Strong Recruiter Performance Management and Accountability in Place

Before you spend one more dollar on technology, you need to get your arms around what your recruiters and sourcers are actually doing and delivering on a daily, weekly, and monthly basis. This starts at a much more basic level than looking at how your days-to-fill metrics are moving. (Oh, boy, don't get me started on how worthless time-to-fill metrics are—that's in Chapter 12.)

As recruiting leaders, we need to build out those activities that lead to hires, and then measure those activities by recruiter. If a recruiter is doing all those things, and those things are leading to a number of hires determined to be successful, they get rewarded in some way. If they aren't, there must be development and consequences for underperforming to the level that is expected.

It's Performance Management 101, and as TA leaders, we tend to suck at basic performance management. We suck at it not because we are bad leaders, but because we haven't slowed down and taken the time to figure out what a successful recruiter looks like. What do these successful recruiters do and deliver? Then, how do we ensure everyone works to get to that same level?

How to Achieve the Greatest ROI from Your TA Technology

Every time you purchase technology for your department, you believe it's going to be awesome. It's the latest and greatest and it's going to change our world. Then, a year later, reality sets in and it seems like every other piece of tech we've bought and it didn't do anything like we had hoped.

Another weakness we have as HR and TA leaders is we tend to support and bring technology solutions with us when we move to new companies. "Well, this technology worked great for me in my last job, so when I get to the new job, I'm going to bring it with me again." This scenario happens constantly, and HR and TA vendors count on this happening for future revenue.

The crazy part of this behavior is that usually the HR and TA tech you are inheriting is completely fine. There's nothing wrong with it; it's just not something you are familiar with, or maybe the last leader didn't do a great job at implementing the technology or holding the team accountable for using it.

The best way to achieve a great ROI on your technology investment is to double down on it when you take on a new position. The first thing I do when taking on a new TA role is to not buy new technology, but ensure my current organization becomes the poster child of using the current technology. We become "super" users of our current tech.

Sometimes that means reimplementation, retraining, or usually both. It also means we are going to have a lot of getting reacquainted meetings with our current technology vendors for the sole purpose of telling them we are their new super users, they just don't know it yet.

Becoming their best customers and super users of their product first lets me know if we have the right technology but just don't realize it yet. It also lets me see what my team has done, or hasn't done, to make this solution successful. If I buy a new solution, I still have the same team to support it. If they aren't prepared to support *this* solution, why would they support a new solution?

Unfortunately, ego gets in the way with most technology purchases. It's not that the new solution is truly superior, but the new solution is *your* solution. If we are new in the role, we often feel the need to do this to show our executives that we know what we're doing. "Hey, the technology sucks, so I'm going to bring in a new solution and fix everything."

Strategically, that may not be a bad way to go. A new technology solution often takes months and years to implement, so this new solution buys you time to fix everything else. The problem, though, is it's frequently just a colossal waste of resources that could be used in so many better ways.

The better strategy would be to bring your CEO and CFO a plan to first determine if the technology you have is usable in the near-future, then tell them the plan for the resources you need in other areas (new career site, branding, extra headcount, etc.). This shows your executive team you're cautious about using your resources but still leaves you an out later on in case you truly do need new tech.

Every applicant tracking system (ATS) does basically 80 percent of the same stuff, but most TA leaders come in and want to "fix" that foundational piece of their stack. So, you buy a new ATS that does basically 90 percent of what the old ATS does. Is that really a great use of your resources?

Great TA leaders and teams are built by using the limited resources you have in the most efficient manner. Sometimes that means turning your current tech into the "new" tech you need by leveraging your tech vendors in a way where they become true partners and want to work with you at a higher level.

Technology vendors are just like anyone else. They love supporting the clients who love their tech, who want to do the most with their tech, and who show them new ways to use their tech that no one has ever thought of. The way you achieve great ROI with your TA technology is to work with your vendors in this way. You'll be amazed at how much more you can get for your team and your organization.

Building Your TA Tech Stack

I've been saying "TA tech stack" quite a bit without really explaining what the heck a "stack" is. In the technology industry, your "stack" is all of those technologies you use to do your work in your organization or department.

Overall, in HR, your tech stack includes human resources information system (HRIS), learning management system (LMS), payroll, and more. It's every system you use on a daily basis to do anything you do. If you line them all up or "stack" them, you get your tech stack. It may be a bit more technical than that, but for the most part that's a pretty easy way to explain your tech stack.

The talent acquisition (TA) technology stack was traditionally pretty simple. You had the applicant tracking system (ATS), email, and phone. Two decades ago, that was the TA tech stack for almost every organization under the enterprise level.

The TA tech stack has grown now to include well over a dozen pieces of technology in the average shop, or up to twenty-five different technologies in the most advanced TA departments. The question becomes, Does this number continue to grow in the future, or does it begin to shrink as many of the small TA technologies begin to combine with others?

It seems like the larger your organization, the stronger the pull is to use just one umbrella system in your shop. We see this in HR as well, with organizations using systems like Workday, Ultimate Software, SAP, Oracle, or Ceridian, which are all large enterprise HRIS systems that are designed to be all-in-one solutions.

While large enterprise all-in-one solutions are designed to look like one piece of technology, they really are just many solutions built together under one user experience and a consistent user interface to make it look like it's one piece of technology. The benefit of using these types of solutions is that usually you're pulling data from the same source because the system is designed to share everything across the platform. Have your eyes glazed over yet?

HR and TA technology are complex, but it's not too complex for you to understand well enough to become the expert in your organization when it comes to making the buy decision on what technology solution fits your organization the best. In most organizations, this decision still lies with information technology (IT), and that has to change. As a talent acquisition leader, you should be the TA expert in your organization, which means you know best what solutions will help solve the problems you have, not someone in IT who has no idea about these issues.

The foundation, currently, of every TA shop is the applicant tracking system. The question then becomes, What should your ATS have, and not have, to make it effective and to make it great?

Like its counterpart, the HRIS, the ATS is your system of record for your organization of applicants. For many organizations, especially those working with local, state, and federal governments or getting funds from government programs, it is especially important that your ATS ensures you remain compliant with your hiring practices as it relates to those rules, laws, and regulations we must all follow.

At this point in the ATS life cycle, they all do this pretty well. The companies selling ATS technology know this is a must-have for all organizations, so this isn't something you really need to be worried about when purchasing this type of technology, and it's fairly easy to check for this compliance when you demo the ATS.

What I'm looking for when I demo a new ATS is the workflow they were built around. Once I see the ATS's apply path for potential employees, it allows me to look at my own processes and see what will work easily within the system, and what won't. I can then make the decision on whether I believe the workflow designed is better than my own, or similar enough that I can adopt those processes. Remember, the last thing I want to do is change the technology, because it works best as it's designed to work.

I'm looking for some basic functionality within the ATS, in even the most inexpensive technology. Does it allow me to run a career site where

I can post my jobs and have applicants apply? Does it allow me to adjust that apply process by position? I may want to have certain filters in place for jobs with a high volume of applicants, but fewer filters for those jobs I will struggle to get applicant flow for.

I'm also looking at how the ATS system communicates with my recruiters and allows my recruiters to communicate with candidates. Do my recruiters need to leave the ATS to send emails and text messages to candidates? Does the system alert my recruiters via email or text when a new candidate applies? Does the ATS system track all communications between my recruiters and candidates?

If you don't normally work as a recruiter, or haven't ever worked as a recruiter, but now you lead the recruiting function, you don't really understand how important it is to easily be able to communicate and track communications within the recruiting process from applicant, to recruiter, to hiring manager and to anyone else who gets involved in your recruiting process. If the system doesn't track it, it didn't happen.

Within this communication, the better ATS system will allow your recruiters to have mass communication abilities as well. If I fill a position and want to disposition all the rest who applied, will the ATS allow me to do this in one step, to all candidates who didn't get the job? Can I quickly and easily with minimal steps communicate to all or part of a list of candidates about next steps within the hiring process?

I need my ATS to reduce administrative steps within my hiring process that cause my team to spend an abnormal amount of time but deliver little value to the entire process. I don't want my recruiters playing the middle person when trying to set up interview times between candidates and hiring managers. My ATS should be able to do this.

Of course, my ATS should give me metrics and analytics, and I'll get into the details of what those should be in Chapter 12, but it's safe to say that I need to be able to pull data on positions, applicant flow, recruiter activity, and so on. I want to be able to pull data from every part of our hiring process, and my ATS is the core to all of that data. This becomes very difficult when you start "bolting" on pieces of talent acquisition technology to your ATS, and while you can probably get them to all work together, getting all that data from disparate systems becomes another monster entirely.

Finally, I need my ATS to close the deal. We found the candidate we want to hire, now let's onboard that candidate and ensure nothing happens between offer acceptance to start date. Sometimes your ATS will have onboarding, sometimes it will be held within your HRIS, and sometimes neither one will have it and you'll have to use a separate onboarding technology.

I actually prefer that my ATS does my onboarding for the simple fact that if my recruiters are doing a great job, I want that relationship to continue until the start date. At this point in the process, no one in the organization knows the candidate as well as the recruiter (or at least it should be that way) and introducing someone else into the mix doesn't make sense.

Too often, organizations bring HR into the mix for onboarding and then something happens (counteroffer, cold feet, etc.) and HR doesn't have the information, or the relationship, in place to save the hire. In my experience, day one is the best day to introduce the HR representative that the person will be working with, a nice handoff from the recruiter. I love to have my recruiters be the first person the new employees see on day one. That familiarity helps everything go smoothly.

Even the best ATS systems can't do everything. You will find some that are great at offering you a wonderful career site interface and great job posting capability, but weak on candidate communication. Or, they've built in great candidate relationship management (CRM) functionality to communicate with candidates, but candidate search is weak. Almost every organization has to make choices when it comes to ATS selection. Even an unlimited budget cannot get you everything.

So, the entire reason we have a TA tech stack is that our foundational piece of technology, the ATS, has perceived weak spots. I say "perceived" because the people who built your ATS did not design it to have weak spots. It has weak spots for you, but it did not have weak spots for the original type of or specific organization it was designed for.

Of course, the more money in your budget, the more choices you'll have across the ATS landscape, which will then give you more options and get you closer to meeting all of your needs. But these holes in the ATS technology are why we have an entire multibillion-dollar talent acquisition technology industry. You started using your ATS and at some point, you said, "Hey, you know what would be great? If our ATS could do X."

And this one statement is how every single piece of talent acquisition technology is built.

What Talent Acquisition Technology Should Be in My Tech Stack?

Can I get basic for a minute?

We tend to get really techy when we start talking about developing and building tech stacks, but I think most TA leaders like us probably aren't that techy. We just want to know what tech we should get and how we should use that tech to get our organizations the best talent. Do you agree with that?

That means the basic TA tech stack is roughly

- ATS,
- Digital phone system, and
- Email.

It can't really get more basic than that, and to be real honest, it's the tech stack that most TA pros use today, still. Add in some job board technology and you probably cover the vast majority of TA shops on the planet.

The one thing you may be asking yourself is, "Do we have a digital phone system?" and, "Why the heck does it matter if our phone system is digital?"

I'm unlike most TA leaders, especially on the corporate side of talent acquisition. Most corporate TA leaders do not track recruiter activity, and I'm the exact opposite. I believe, with my entire being, that recruiting, similar to sales, is an activity-driven profession. Teach the right activities, measure those activities, refine and develop those activities, and amazing things can happen for you in finding talent.

The one activity that is foundational for recruiting is making a phone call to a candidate. Thus, you need a digital phone system that allows you to track recruiter phone activity via software that you can usually purchase from the company who sold you your phones, or any other sales-related technology vendor.

Your ATS should track email activity, and some may even track phone activity, but it is essential to put this in place and start building out baselines for your team so you know how much activity equals each kind of hire you make. The great part about call-tracking software is that it is rather inexpensive and easy to use.

You'll be shocked at how little activity is actually taking place, which is a good thing. I recommend setting up the call-tracking software without your recruiters knowing it's there and let it run for a month. You need to know what is actually happening, for real, before you can set out to make changes, so this true baseline is very important.

After getting your baseline, you can then find positive ways to increase this activity and develop training to help your recruiters get better at all parts of screening and closing candidates. The tracking software is not set up as a disciplinary, micromanaging hammer. It's there to show how much activity it takes to make one placement, which allows you to build out how big your team should be, what technology will help you do it faster, and your annual budget.

Enough of the basics. Let's get into the cool technology that can help your talent acquisition department run like it's on steroids.

This is where I could geek out for one hundred pages, but I'm really going to limit myself to a few technologies that I believe every single TA shop should be using, and the ones I know to have the best return on investment. Understand that the technology landscape is changing very quickly and before this book is even published, some cool new tech will be on the market that isn't mentioned here.

All, or most, of these technologies may also be a part of your current ATS. I'm really doubtful your ATS will have all of these, but across all ATSs, most will incorporate a certain level of the technologies discussed next. Many ATS vendors will tell you they have X technology, but what they really have is a very light or watered-down version of a technology meant to look like the one you really want—the old bait and switch. As I say this, though, some ATS vendors that have built their platforms in the past few years are getting sophisticated in what they are offering, so there's hope.

Employee Referral Automation (ERA)

Employee referral automation has been around for almost a decade. It was first launched as a stand-alone technology by Jobvite. (Jobvite has since built a complete ATS as well.) Since Jobvite's launch, many companies have entered the employee referral automation space. The concept of employee referral automation is fairly simple, which makes it brilliant.

Employee referrals make up one of our top sources of hire. Also, employee referrals tend to be our number-one source for top quality of hires. So, wouldn't we all want more employee referrals? The answer is yes!

The problem was the employee referral programs we developed and launched internally usually sucked and died slow, painful deaths on the wall of the break room. They were hard to administer and even harder to maintain and keep going. ERA changed all of that by developing a technology that does all of this for you, plus more.

Great ERA software allows you to easily send your new job openings to all, or a segment of, your employees, who can then, with one click, share this job with their social networks via LinkedIn, Facebook, X (formerly known as Twitter), and so on. Those friends of the employee can then share it with their friends with one click as well.

Eventually, the referral will come back to your recruiting team and the ERA software lets your team know which employee started the referral share, so you can reward that employee for helping your organization. ERA software also lets you set up scoreboards within the organization, reward different levels of referrals, and reward different activities along the referral life cycle (awareness, prescreen, interview, offer, hire, etc.—you decide).

For my talent acquisition budget, ERA technology has the single greatest return on investment, even with large referral bonuses, and yet, most organizations aren't using it. Most of the technology vendors in the space have shown that using this product will increase your referral hires by 20 percent to 40 percent. The automation alone allows more employees to be involved, in a much easier way. Plus, large referral payouts have been shown to be rather ineffective as a strategy to attract more referrals. If an employee wants to refer a friend, they will; money doesn't really matter.

Sourcing Technology

One other aspect that ATSs are weak in is the ability to source candidates. While they're excellent at processing through applicants who come to your career site or click on a job posting of some sort, they really don't go out and help your recruiters find candidates. We want our recruiters to be hunters, not farmers (well, at least I do!).

Sourcing technology started, like employee referral automation, with a simple concept. We all go out and play and live on the internet. When we do this, we leave stuff behind, kind of like the exhaust your car leaves behind as you drive. This internet exhaust can be collected by various technologies and if it's pieced all together you can start to get a pretty clear picture of who the person is.

You go on LinkedIn, Facebook, or other social sites, or you may be listed on a professional association site for your profession, or maybe you attended a conference or won an award. Sourcing technology will aggregate all of this data and build a profile of you. These profiles will often include email addresses, phone numbers, and other contact information. It's truly amazing how much is out there and how accurate the data are with sourcing technology.

These candidate aggregators allow your recruiters to quickly find talent who don't even know they are about to be found. Over the years, the sourcing technology has evolved to also allow you to search for diversity hires, gender hires, specific universities, locations, competitor companies, and so on.

The technology has gotten so advanced so quickly in this space that it has really affected the entire profession of sourcing. It used to be that organizations would have to hire sourcing specialists trained in Boolean internet search operators who were trained at building search strings to find the candidates you wanted. Now, this technology can do all of that in seconds, using natural language, allowing your recruiters to do most of the work traditional sourcers were hired to do.

The newest versions of sourcing technology have also added in screening components and will even add in your ATS database as part of the full sourcing environment. This is critical as ATSs have traditionally been very weak at search, so all those thousands and millions of candidates who applied to your jobs in the past are not ever being used again.

Most of us are sitting on a massive gold mine of talent in our own ATS database, but we can't ever uncover them. These are candidates who have already said, in the words of Carly Rae Jepson, "Hey, I don't know you, and this is crazy, but call me, maybe!" but we don't. We spend all our resources to get them to apply, then we don't hire them at the time they applied, so we believe they are awful when in reality they hadn't applied for the right job for them or at the right time.

The best sourcing technology on the market will uncover this great talent, again, in your own database, plus include the new applicants, plus bring in profiles of people who don't even know you yet, then rank them for your team so they know who to target first. It's truly an amazing time to be in talent acquisition.

Recruitment Marketing/CRM

Chapter 10 is dedicated to recruitment marketing, but, in this section, I want to speak specifically to the technology behind recruitment marketing. It's one of the fastest-growing segments in the talent acquisition technology space, and some would argue that a recruitment marketing platform is the ATS of the future.

Recruitment marketing technology is mostly built on a CRM backbone. CRM, in talent acquisition, stands for candidate relationship management. What does that mean? Basically, it's sales software that vendors have made some slight adaptations to so it will work in a similar way but with candidates, not sales prospects.

If you truly think about it, each candidate you have is basically a sales prospect. What you are selling them is an opportunity to come work for your company. Just like CRM for sales, you want to stay in front of your candidates, like companies want to stay in front of people who may buy something from them.

At its basic level, CRM is just a big database (much like your ATS) used to automatically communicate to candidates via various rules you put in place. Maybe you want to send a quick update email to every engineer who has applied to your company in the past year, but only those candidates you didn't interview. CRM can do that very easily, and add another email to those who didn't reply a week later. CRM does this at the most basic level, but it can do so much more.

The most robust recruitment marketing platforms also will know when a candidate comes back to your career site but hasn't applied to your job yet. How? Robust platforms are able to recognize a surfer's IP address and to know what the candidate looked at the last time he or she was on your site.

Let's say an engineer from your competitor is looking for a similar job with your company. They will visit your career site and look around. Based on this behavior, a recruitment marketing system can make assumptions that they must be an engineer based on the jobs they are looking at, then tailor specific content on your career site for this individual, without even knowing for sure who they are.

The recruitment marketing platform also can alert one of your recruiters that this candidate is back and looking at "that" engineering job once again, and open up a chat window for your recruiter to try and strike up a conversation and get them to apply.

It's all a little "Big Brother" for some, but I think it's revolutionary for organizations to engage in talent. Having a CRM is critical for talent acquisition to effectively nurture the candidates they have in their ATS and build dynamic, on-demand talent pipelines.

Recruitment marketing technology is complex. It's not something, like our ATSs, that you can just set up once and walk away. It's a technology that needs someone running it, for the most part. While most are user-friendly, you definitely want someone on your team who has an affinity for technology to be the one responsible for it. It's very powerful and has a strong ROI for those organizations that effectively leverage it.

Selection Science and Pre-Hire Technology

I love the latest technology involved in selection science. It used to be that "selection science" meant personality assessments online, but this isn't your father's Oldsmobile! (The funny part about saying that line is most people under 30 have no idea what an Oldsmobile even is!)

When I think about selection science today, I'm thinking about technology that truly tells you why one candidate is better than another. TA technology has become so advanced in its predictive capabilities that best-in-class TA functions should be creating a consistently structured interview, assessment methodology, and framework that more consistently delivers the talent you desire.

This framework would include the traditional competency/behavioral interview, of course, but it also includes re-hire assessments at both the cultural and functional/technical fit level, and it should include a cognitive assessment as well. It never hurt anyone to hire smart people!

I've been fortunate to be a part of a couple of organizations that did pre-hire cognitive assessments at high volume hiring in the hundreds of thousands. What we found consistently is that when given the chance to hire smart people over not-as-smart people with experience, smart people on average fare better in performance in the long run.

When Google looked at the millions of interviews recruiters conducted, it found that interviews, by themselves, were virtually a waste of time.[2] Google found that selecting talent based on just an interview process with no other selection criteria was only 1 percent better than flipping a coin!

The best predictor of success, Google found, was a work sample, at a 29 percent success rate. Work samples, though, are time-consuming and hard to develop. But, there are many technologies on the market that provide virtual work samples, especially in the IT space, that are easy to use and cost-effective.

The next best predictor of candidate success from Google? Cognitive ability, at 26 percent! So, you can begin to see how your success increases as you build out your selection methodology by adding in selection science components. Every segment increases your odds to better select a candidate that will have success in your environment.

Some of the selection science on the market is now using natural language processing science to predict how one candidate is better than another in the pre-hire phase, and the data are scary accurate! This type of technology takes the candidate's online audio or video interview file, and analyzes it before you even see it, then ranks the candidates based on thousands of data points.

You can imagine the amount of data a computer can get from a video file. The words you use, the inflection of your voice, the tone of your voice, the sophistication of your language use, or whether you maintained eye contact. There are over 25,000 different attributes the computer will analyze to come up with a prediction, which helps you narrow down which candidates you should be spending your time on.

Can you imagine how many of those attributes the average human brain picks up on during the interview? Maybe a few dozen! The science will always be smarter than we are as humans, and more consistent in selection. If you create a methodology and religiously follow it and use the technology to help you cull your candidates, you will be amazed at the long-term results in raising the talent in your organization.

Do You Still Check References?

I love asking this question in front of large talent acquisition audiences and teams because the answer should be "yes" 100 percent of the time, right? I usually get about 90 percent of the audience that will raise their hands. That's pretty close to the SHRM research that shows, depending on the role, organizations check between 80 percent and 90 percent of references.[3]

So, then I'll ask, "How do you check references?"

This is where checking references starts to fall apart. Of those 80 percent or 90 percent who check references, around 90 percent of those check references the traditional way that we've checked references for generations.

We ask a candidate to provide us professional references. He gives us three people to call. We call all three people. The three references tell us the candidate walks on water. And we hire him. Heck, my own references are my second-grade teacher, my dad's golfing league partner of twenty years, and a guy I worked with for a decade (I'm also the godfather to his children).

What do you think those three people will say about me? "Yes, Tim is magical and you would be crazy not to hire him!" It's the most likely response!

Sound familiar?

It should; this is the way we've always done it and it's the way most of us will still be doing it a decade from now. The problem with this is it's a waste of time and resources, and it's ineffective.

The next questions I'll ask is, "When was the last time you didn't hire someone based on the reference check?" Crickets. Every once in a while, I'll get a brave soul to say, "Well, three years ago, I had this mother tell me not to hire her son so we didn't." Mom? You talked to Mom for a reference? Most can never recall a time when they didn't hire someone based on a reference.

Checking references became a formality of hiring, but not one that helped us select better talent.

I think every single recruiter who checks references in this manner should stop immediately and never check another reference because the resources you are wasting are massive, and you're getting nothing in return for your effort.

What you should be doing, if you want to check references, is leveraging reference checking technology. Reference checking technology actually will have you not hire about 15 percent of those candidates you want to hire, but the references will tell you that the candidate isn't a good fit for your organization or the job you're about to hire them for. A 15 percent reject rate compared to 0 percent is huge.

Reference checking technology asks the reference, via online survey, to rate a person on a scale of two potential positive choices: Is the candidate a gregarious team player, or are they a thoughtful, insightful, heads-down worker? At which spectrum is the candidate more natural?

The reference then gives you some insight into how this person truly is, and the reference still believes he is giving the candidate a positive reference. What the reference doesn't know is what you're truly looking for from a candidate in your organization for that specific position.

All this leads to you getting an accurate picture of who the candidate is from people who know them best and gives you the best insight to whether you should hire them or not. Also, because this is automated, and reminders are sent automatically when someone doesn't respond, the response rate and turnaround time to completion are high and fast.

Overall, when you combine the technology with the outcome, and the fact your team is no longer doing all of these references manually, the cost savings and ROI are some of the better outcomes in talent acquisition technology.

Talent acquisition technology and your TA tech stack could be an entire book in itself. The industry is changing at a breathtaking pace and new TA tech comes on the market each week. It's our responsibility as leaders to keep up with this. You don't need to know it inside and out, but you need to at least know what's going on with those foundational pieces of your stack that make the most impact on your hiring.

Wait! What About Skills?

Unless you've been living under a rock, you've probably heard of the new "skills" revolution going on in HR technology. The theory behind skills is admirable. For most of recruiting history, we've relied on systems and processes of selection that are filled with all kinds of privilege. Not all people have access to the same education and experiences, which is how most organizations have selected talent for a century or more.

Wouldn't it be better if we just hired based on "skill"?

This is where this concept gets very hard to pull off. In theory, if you wanted to hire based on skill, you would need to know a few things with a high degree of accuracy:

1. What skills do we need for each job we hire?
2. How can we accurately measure each of these skills?
3. How can we determine if a candidate has the skills we need and what level of skill they have?

Without all of this knowledge, hiring by skill doesn't work! I believe the theory behind why we would want to hire by skill is solid, but in practice, it's extremely hard and expensive to pull off.

The other piece around hiring for skill is that you just don't hire skills. You hire humans. Humans come with all kinds of experiences that can be very valuable to the job and the organization. You might have graduated college and that gave you an amazing network of bright people who you can leverage when you need something. You might have worked at some amazing companies that gave you experience working on things only employees of that company could have worked on. You might have been raised by a single mom who demonstrated to you an unparalleled work ethic.

We are not a list of verifiable skills. We are robust, unique humans full of skills, experiences, backgrounds, and different levels of learning agility.

You will most likely be asked to use or look at skills technology. If you use large human capital management (HCM) systems it's already built into the platform. I just urge you to be cautious on skills-based hiring. I believe, if done accurately and thoroughly, it can, without a doubt, help you in selection, but it will be extremely difficult to do in all positions across your organization. And, just like education and experience should only be limiting factors in selection, skills are just one more factor to consider.

Here's the thing . . .

Most recruiting technology that was built in the last ten years or so is fairly decent. You can win with it. Use it as it's designed. Don't ask the vendor to break it (err . . . customize it). Force your team to become superusers of your technology. Always remember, if you suck at recruiting, great recruiting technology will allow you to suck much faster. Fix your sh*t internally before you worry about tech.

» 10 «

If You Build It, Talent Will Come!

So, we've talked about building a great team, and we've built a talent acquisition tech stack that will be industry leading, now let's turn on the marketing machine!

"Perception is reality" is a common phrase we hear used in so many areas of our life, and never more than in recruitment marketing (RM) and employment branding (EB). The reality in RM and EB is that most of us offer basically the same work experience as everyone else.

We have a good work environment, not great. We offer good pay, benefits, and workmates, but it's very similar to most other organizations. We'll give you decent career development, but nothing too special. We live in a society where almost all of us are virtually the same when it comes to work experience and opportunity.

That's the reality. We are more alike at work than we are different. This is why recruitment marketing and employment branding are so critical to your success of attracting noticeably better talent to your organization.

I don't know about you, but I'm mostly a sucker when it comes to marketing. I love to think that I'm not sold easily, but I am.

I love to think that when I buy that Patagonia puffer jacket for $259 that it's going to be exceptionally better than the off-brand puffer jacket for $99. It's not, but I just love that Patagonia brand! I feel like somehow, I'm helping the world by buying Patagonia. That wearing that Patagonia jacket will give me some sort of experience that others are not getting.

Do you know what that "experience" is? That's great marketing!

What's the difference, then, between recruitment marketing and employment branding? Is there a difference between these two functions?

To be sure, recruitment marketing and employment branding within talent acquisition (TA) often get used interchangeably by most of us. Tracy Parsons, vice president of recruitment marketing, Center of Excellence at SmashFly Technologies, gives a great example of the subtle differences:[1]

Recruitment Marketing:

Working for our company is amazing, you should apply!

Recruitment Advertising:

Apply now.

Apply now.

Apply now.

Employer Branding:

I've heard your company is amazing, where do I apply?

Parson says:

> When we look at how all these concepts fit together, it comes down to how, and to whom, you're communicating and differentiating your message.
>
> For instance, when you're developing an employer brand, it's critical that it is:
>
> - Fundamentally based on who you really are as an employer.
> - True, defensible, and authentic.
> - Reflected in how your audience perceives you as well.

It's impossible to build an employer brand without an external narrative. In fact, in our highly digital, social, and review-crazed world that external narrative likely fuels more influence than the internal narrative. Good employer brands marry the two; the best employer brands find and communicate the right story internally so that it becomes the external story.

Parsons says, and I completely agree, "Recruitment marketing brings your employer brand to life!"

It's not an either-or scenario. You need both to be successful in getting your message out to candidates. The critical failure most organizations make in having a successful employment brand is allowing their strategy to disregard the importance of getting this message out to candidates in a way they want to consume.

Every organization has an employment brand. Yours may not be well-known within the marketplace, but it doesn't mean that your brand isn't any more engaging than the most successful employment brands in the world.

What I see in the candidate marketplace is that the best employment brands are usually backed by great recruitment marketing. I constantly find exceptional employment brands that no one has ever heard of, and the leadership always says the exact same thing: "Tim! Yeah, we are actually that great and our people love us; we just need for candidates to know what we already know."

It's very common for organizations to have wonderful attributes of being a great place to work. Stories that make you laugh and cry. Environments that make you feel welcomed, encouraged, and challenged. Yet, no one outside of that organization has any idea.

This is the ultimate challenge we face with employment branding and recruitment marketing. We love to spend time building our employment brand and story; we usually don't like to brag about ourselves. Do more bragging! Don't stop bragging! You'll get sick of hearing yourself say the same thing over and over, but that millionth time you say it may just be the first time that "perfect" candidate hears it for the first time.

Recruit Me Like You Mean It!

By now you've figured out I'm not overly sophisticated when it comes to talent acquisition strategy. I probably see things a bit differently than most in talent acquisition, as I do not think what we do is overly complicated. Most of talent acquisition is basic human psychology and behavior, repeated over and over.

When it comes to your employment brand, I also like to keep it simple. The simplest messages resonate faster and longer with candidates. We all have some simple and positive things to tell candidates about our organizations, our jobs, and our culture.

Even after all of this, we have to believe that this story, our employment brand, matters. If it doesn't matter to candidates, then why is there so much focus on this concept? Maybe the bigger question for candidates is, What matters first?

Does a candidate first hear about your brand and then want to know more? Or does a candidate find out about your jobs through another means, then want to learn more about who you really are? Does it matter which one hooks them first when it comes to finally landing that candidate?

I've been around college athletics most of my life. My wife was an NCAA Division I (D1) college volleyball player. I was an assistant coach, which is how I met her. We have three sons, two of whom have gone on to play college athletics. Recruiting in college athletics is a really strange beast.

The majority of high school athletes have a dream to play at the next level of their given sport of choice. There are very few elite high school athletes that will be recruited in a major way. These are the stories we see on TV and read about in the news. The five-star kid can lift a truck and Nick Saban is coming to the house for dinner next week to talk him into coming to the University of Alabama.

The reality is much less glamorous for most kids who play college athletics. For most athletes, the experience is closer to the job-seeking experience. The athlete (job seeker) wants to play at the next level and needs to find a college who wants them.

While most of us think about college athletics as the big-time college football we see on Saturdays or the NCAA basketball tournament, the vast amount of college athletes participate at lower levels. There are thousands of colleges at the DI, DII, DIII, NAIA (National Association of Intercollegiate Athletics), and junior college (JUCO) ranks that need these athletes to fill their sports teams.

You can think of these levels like the employer landscape. The Big Three automotive companies represent DI schools, then you have automotive suppliers at the DII and DIII levels, and the tier-two suppliers to the automotive companies are the NAIA and JUCO levels. If you truly want to work in the automotive industry, your eventual goal is probably working for one of the major automotive companies.

So, this becomes a matchmaking endeavor. An athlete needs to find a college that wants them, and colleges need to find the best talent available to come to their institutions to participate. On the outside, this seems like a fairly transactional process. You have a pool of athletes at each sport, and you have a pool of positions at colleges, and through the selection process, colleges and athletes will make their choices.

One pretty cool thing happens in this recruiting process and it's the most basic raw human emotion. Most of us want to be wanted by others. I've seen this play out a number of times with athletes and coaches. Both sides want to be wanted. Of course, athletes love to be recruited by coaches who make them feel special. Also, college coaches want to know that they are the first choice of the athletes.

What I've seen happen is an athlete will take a position at a college that may be a bit lower level than they probably could play at, all because a coach shows them how much they are actually wanted by that college. Also, coaches will take players who may be a little less than they can get because the kid has shown that the coaches' institution is their number-one choice.

We do this because we want to be wanted. We all want to be recruited by someone who truly wants us. Nobody wants to be your second choice, and you don't want to be a backup plan for a candidate. This is why, as TA professionals, we lose our mind when a candidate says they want to "think about it." What do you have to think about? I love you! You love me! We are meant for each other! Or so we hoped.

One of my sons accepted a position to play baseball at a junior college when he had offers in hand from higher institutions, and it was simply that the coach did his homework and was prepared more than any other coach when my son visited the college. He felt wanted. He felt the coach really did research to understand what he was looking for, even though that college had fewer facilities and wasn't as attractive as other offers.

Never discount the single greatest power you have in recruitment marketing. We hold the power to show someone they are desired by our organization, by our hiring managers, that hiring them can make a difference. It's such a powerful emotion and feeling that can make people do some crazy things. Think about all those losers in your life you've dated simply because they made you feel special!

This is one of the core elements of your recruitment marketing practice. We make people feel wanted by how we pursue them. That one boy who asked you out a hundred times, but acted like a stalker, didn't win your heart. But another boy who worked to understand what you liked, was perceptive to your strengths, and then called you a hundred times did win your heart!

Sounds easy enough. Pursue aggressively, but not so aggressively that candidates get creeped out. We do this by being transparent and honest about our intentions. We do this by building trust and sharing information that is important to the candidate. We do this by making the experience personal to them. No one wants to be a number. They want to be *the* number.

Just like we would want to be recruited, candidates want us to recruit them in the same way—like we mean it.

Employment Branding on a Budget!

We tend to think employment branding—great employment branding—takes a ton of resources. We are also told that it's really difficult and you probably need outside help. Some of the largest corporations spend a low amount on employment branding, and they have strong employment brands.

Most employment branding experts that you engage spend most of their time helping you take off your own blinders to your own great stories. It's not about creating your story; it's about a third person coming in with no preconceived ideas and pointing out the stories that are right in front of your face.

I'm not disparaging outside branding consultants. Some of my best, most brilliant friends are in the employment branding space and do exceptional work. I think you can do really good employment branding on your own if you have the capacity and desire. If you don't, that's when outside help can be a godsend.

There are a number of questions you need to ask of your organization and department before starting down this path. Shaunda Zilich, employment branding leader at General Electric (GE), is one of the top employment branding minds anywhere and she likes to ask these questions:[2]

- What resources do I have? (Tech, people, budget, buy-in, etc.)
- What does success look like?
- How do I use my resources correctly?
- What's our strategy? (Write it down.)
- How will I implement the strategy?

Zilich says it's good to interview those in leadership, TA, and marketing to understand their understanding of employment branding and how you fit together as well as to create buy-in. The buy-in is critical as you build your employment brand. You need these key stakeholders to be champions as well.

So, I told you not to listen to unicorns and then I go and bring in a unicorn company like GE and a rock star like Zilich to talk about employment branding, but there's something you need to know. Zilich started GE's employment brand with exactly zero dollars in her budget.

One of the largest and most successful companies in the world started its employment branding function on a shoestring budget. How? Employment branding at its core is just a story, and your best stories are those of your employees.

Think about all the great stories you've heard in your organizations. The great customer service stories, the great client stories where everyone went above and beyond, and the great team stories of your employees taking care of each other. Sometimes it gets overwhelming because you have so many.

The best employment brands are built out of these stories. By the way, all those stories are free. You didn't have to pay a marketing agency to make them up. They're real and raw, and completely who you are. What's great about being who you are in your employment brand is that you will attract candidates who are or want to be just like you. It makes cultural fit a fairly easy hurdle to get over when that happens.

So many organizations fail at employment branding. I asked Zilich why this happens. Why do organizations fail at something that is honestly just the ability to reflect yourself back to a candidate? Here's her answer:

> Strategy versus doing. It is important to have both, but you need to decide what resources you have in doing so. A lot of times I see companies hiring someone to run EB just to promote and "do their social channels." This is one part of EB; however, it is so much more. The strategy needs to be simple, robust, and yet fluid as TA transforms and marketing becomes a larger part of the process. The strategy needs to include the resources dedicated to the "doing" to carry it out.[3]

Never underestimate the value of someone who can execute your strategy. Great strategies die in conference rooms because no one on the team can figure out how to execute. Great employment branding is this combination of developing your story (EB) and ensuring your message gets in front of the right people, at the right time (RM).

I run the TransfoRM Facebook group that caters to and shares insights every day on recruitment marketing. (If you're in HR and TA and you're not leveraging Facebook groups to develop and educate yourself, you're missing out. Big time! So many great professionals, freely sharing great advice every day.) There are hundreds of the top recruitment marketing and employment branding experts in that group. So, I posted this question to them:

> "Hey, I'm writing a book on TA and a chapter on recruitment marketing. What can't I leave out?"

I got dozens of comments with great pieces of advice I wanted to share. This would be like if you could have ten or twelve of the top employment branding experts sitting down in front of you and sharing their best advice. This is what these experts had to say:

Don't be safe with your content. Take some risks and have some fun. Put it all out there so people can opt out if the culture is not for them.

—Audra Knight, recruitment operations manager, Tenable Network Security

Don't pick one channel. Diversify your investments. Also, measure the funnel. Just because a bunch of people go into the top doesn't mean they're quality.

—Katrina Kibben, employer branding, Randstad Sourceright

People appreciate real and refreshing over corporate and cookie cutter. And don't forget to activate your brand and messaging internally. Keep recruiting your internal employees for retention and mobility.

—Jess Von Bank, vice president, market engagement, Symphony Talent

Budget. We have crossed into a realm where bootstrapping is not going to cut it. Also, test, fail fast, adjust, or pivot. Last, TA buy-in/alignment, too many RM shops operate in a silo.

—Holland Dombeck, director of employment branding, ADP

Hire fans, not candidates.

—Steve Ward, talent attraction strategy, GovNow

Be prepared to educate internal stakeholders over and over and over in multiple ways so your story becomes their story. Bring them along.

—Dina Medeiros, director of talent and employment branding, HoYoverse

EB is really focused on the overall reputation and brand of the company as an employer. It's more long term. RM is more tied to the real-time hiring goals of the organization and typically tied to a call to action rather than general raising of awareness. Also, create a test and learn culture by embracing failure as a product of innovation!

—Will Staney, founder, Proactive Talent Strategies

Consistent, compelling communication and relevant nurture over time—that's truly how marketing becomes effective for sales and it'll be the same for recruitment marketing. Timing is everything, even more so in careers!

—Elyse Mayer, director of content, Smashfly Technologies

Isn't that wonderful advice? You see all the synergies come out when you see the best in the business talk about employment branding and recruitment marketing. It's about finding your story, creating great content to engage your target audience, and doing it over and over, so your future hires will know what to expect from your organization. Then you deliver on that employment branding promise.

Your Free Employment Branding and Recruitment Marketing People Machine

There are a couple of other folks I need to introduce to you before I tell you a little more about something really cool GE's Shaunda Zilich did: Lars Schmidt, founder of Amplify Talent and former HR leader at NPR, and Ambrosia Vertesi, vice president of people at Duo Security and former vice president of talent at Hootsuite.

Lars and Ambrosia started the organization called HR Open Source (HROS.co). The concept was, What if HR and TA pros worked the same way developers and software engineers in technology work with open source software? At its simplest terms, open source software is free for everyone, and everyone can work on it and help build it out. Everyone works on creating something everyone else can use, and it's all volunteered.

HR Open Source is the same idea but for us HR and TA nerds! We all need to build the same kinds of programs. We all have limited budgets. Why aren't we all working together and sharing our work for others to add to it, make it better, then sharing it all back to the community again?

Currently, there are thousands of HR Open Source members all over the world sharing their work and helping each other. Zilich at GE is one of those people who shared what may be the single best employment branding and recruitment marketing idea ever.

Zilich's idea was basically, What if we could take all those employees in our organization who happen to love working for our company and couldn't wait to share their love with their networks? You may only have a handful of these "super" employees; some organizations, like GE, may have thousands! The power of our people, banded together, under one cause could do some really cool stuff!

This is how GE developed their digital brand ambassador program, to match talent with opportunity. Remember, when Zilich started at GE, she had virtually no budget, but what she did have was a lot of GE employees who loved being GE employees!

GE's program went from a handful to over 13,000 employees helping to connect GE's new digital brand to a broader audience of candidates through social amplification strategies, and just good old-fashion sharing of great content.

The key for GE was to first get the key stakeholders involved that you actually had a little bit of influence over: your other talent acquisition and HR friends within the company. This is all voluntary, so you need to start with a smaller group that you know will not only be excited to launch but keep it going as well.

There's one crazy thing that will happen if you decide to go down this path of launching a brand ambassador program: your volunteers will ask a question that you probably never even thought of, "Are you sure the company is okay with us doing this?" They're asking if they have permission.

Step back and think about that concept for a minute. Why do our own employees think they need permission to share great content about our company, our brand, about how great it is to work for your organization? Why would anyone question that?

We (HR) did that to them. Our leadership did that to them. Our legal teams have done this to them. Our employees are scared for their jobs if they share anything publicly about the company they work for, and it's so bad that even when we ask them to share clearly positive content, they will still ask the question!

That's your first hurdle. It's not a big one, but it's one that always makes me pause for a bit and think how messed up corporate America can get.

The easiest part of a brand ambassador program is the launch, but longevity is the key to success, and Zilich and GE definitely built this factor into their strategy. One of the first things she did was build a one-hour training session for all those brand ambassadors who volunteered.

The basic rundown of the one-hour training is as follows:

- Why?
- Win/win—professional branding for you and (if you choose) GE.
- Being safe online.
- Maximizing your LinkedIn profile.
- The art of storytelling; your "why."
- Other places you can "hang out online"—social, review, content sites.
- Resources.[4]

From this training agenda, you can see that developing your corporate story is a critical first piece that you have to be ready to share, but you also have to help your employees develop their brand story as well. What is it about working for your organization, in that specific role, that is special for them?

Not only are these volunteers helping you spread your employment brand to a much broader audience in a very transparent and authentic way, but you are also helping them develop their own personal brand. That's part of the deal. You're going to help us, but we are also going to help you.

The time commitment and the "how" is truly up to the volunteers. The basic time commitment of social sharing of content may only take ten minutes of each week, and they choose the platforms they prefer to use. It may be Facebook, LinkedIn, X (formerly known as Twitter), Instagram, Snapchat, and so on. This "natural" selection of social sharing adds to the transparency of your brand ambassador program.

For those leading the program (and remember GE is a company of over 350,000 employees, and this started with one person—Zilich), their job is to curate and create content for your ambassadors to share.

When Zilich first started she would send a weekly email out to a small group of ambassadors with some simple instructions to share. This doesn't have to be super sophisticated to start, but you do need to plan out your program and strategy. You want to be very consistent in your approach and know it will start small and slowly, and build.

I love this approach to employment branding and recruitment marketing because it involves both disciplines completely, as well as those employees who are your biggest fans, which is the most underutilized asset we have in talent acquisition. This isn't an exclusive program, either. While it starts out small, the key is attracting other employees to come in and become an ambassador as well, and that should also be built into your strategy.

We all have these employees who love working for us, and now we finally have a way to engage them in an active program to help the organization in a major way. There may not be a better win-win program ever launched in the history of TA.

Design Matters

There is a concept called "design thinking," which is a methodology used by designers to solve complex problems and find desirable solutions for clients. A design mindset is not problem focused, it's solution focused and action oriented toward creating a preferred future. Design thinking draws on logic, imagination, intuition, and systemic reasoning to explore possibilities of what could be—and to create desired outcomes that benefit the end user (the customer).[5]

Tim Brown (CEO of IDEO) says, "Design thinking can be described as a discipline that uses the designer's sensibility and methods to match people's needs with what is technologically feasible and what a viable business strategy can convert into customer value and market opportunity."[6]

In HR, our first action is usually not solution focused, it's problem focused, and we tend to never think about our "preferred" future. We're pragmatic by nature as a function. We've been trained to be this way, mostly because of all the rules and laws we must concern ourselves with in our profession to help mitigate risk for our organizations.

The thing is, candidates don't care about how we want to do our jobs. They only care about what they want. That's just a reality we all live with and understand. We want to control candidate behavior much like we try to control employee behavior, but they don't work for us, so it never works out well for us!

The one thing we know is that design is having a huge effect on candidate behavior. Your brand and your culture can no longer just be an awesome place to work. Candidates now also want it to look like an awesome place to work. The visual and environmental aspects of who and what they'll be working with has become important to much of the younger workforce.

Newer generations entering the workforce and already in the workforce grew up in a visual world. They have an expectation that they'll be working in an environment like all those cool workplaces they've seen on TV, online, and so on. This is an actual challenge for talent acquisition, and one most of us are just not prepared for.

Before you say to yourself, "Ugh, those millennials!" understand design plays a huge role in how we all make decisions. No one wants to work in a 1980s cube with beige walls and beige carpet and fluorescent lighting. For generations, most of us just figured this was what the work environment was supposed to be and that there was nothing we could do about it, so we showed up and mostly hated it, but didn't talk about it.

A couple of decades ago the office furniture industry got together and decided we all would be way more productive if we worked in open-office environments, and we started tearing down the walls and cubes in our workplaces. While the open-office concept had little to do with productivity, and much more to do with selling new office furniture lines (hello, marketing at its finest!), we all learned that there were way cooler office designs to be had.

So, we know design matters when it comes to work environments for most of our candidates, but design also matters when it comes to everything else within our employment brand we touch as well: our career site, collateral materials, career fair displays, and email templates.

Of course, we want our employment brand design to match and coordinate with our corporate brand. So, if your corporate brand design sucks, you're in trouble right off the bat. But, usually, our corporate brand is more on point, and it's our own employment brand that needs work on catching up.

For decades, in HR and TA, we've cut-and-pasted our way to try and make up something that looks kind of like our corporate brand for recruiting but was never exactly the way we wanted it to be. All this has to stop. The time has come when our marketing team no longer can push employment branding design down the list of priorities. If talent is a priority in your organization then employment branding design also is a priority in your organization.

If your own marketing team can't help you, you need to get a budget from your executives to hire a professional agency to get you up to speed. That isn't a nice-to-have kind of thing; that's priority number one. You have candidates stopping by every day, looking at your organization and they're saying, "Um, no!" It takes them roughly three seconds to make that determination because your design sucks. They're not even hearing your story because your design sucks.

I'll go so far as to say that I would rather have great design than great stories. If we are talking about talent attraction, design will get them in the door, and if it's truly great design, many will stay, believing any organization that has such great design must have great stories, or eventually they will because everyone will want to work at your company.

This is hard buy-in for many older executives that will tell you war stories of working in the garage on a broken chair with only three wheels and a hole in the roof. No one cares about your war stories! Our competition is kicking our butts for talent because we look like a drab place to work.

Ask yourself, would you rather walk into a Target or a Walmart?

You have the choice; they're right next to each other. Brand new Target, brand new Walmart: which one are you drawn in to check out first? I shop at both, but I'll always check out the Target first because design wins. Design wins over function every single time. Of course, ideally, we want both, but never discount the force great design can be for your employment brand.

Active versus Passive Candidates

Every year, LinkedIn conducts a Global Talent Trends Survey of more than 26,000 professionals, and in the past year more than 7,000 have changed jobs.[7] It's a fascinating insight into the mind of candidates and why they choose one job over another.

We've been conditioned for decades to believe there are two types of candidates, passive and active. Active means those candidates who are out aggressively trying to find their next job. They may be posting their résumés on job boards, updating their LinkedIn profile, applying for jobs online, and so on. Passive candidates, then, are folks who are not looking for a new job.

Our hiring managers are then conditioned to believe, for some crazy reason, that passive candidates are a higher quality candidate than active candidates. The theory is that if you're actively searching for a job, you must suck for some reason. Let's just say, this belief by our hiring managers isn't well thought through.

IBM's Smarter Workforce Institute in 2017 found that higher performers are much more likely to be attracted to newer jobs because they are more actively searching out higher-level skill development and more responsibility.[8] So, this would indicate that a good percentage of those actively searching for jobs are probably considered high performers in their current organizations.

Regardless, the LinkedIn survey tells us that this entire concept of passive and active is basically a load of crap. Its survey has consistently found that 90 percent of the entire workforce is open to hearing about new opportunities. That makes 90 percent of us active. Those last 10 percent you'll never hire anyway because those are the folks who are close to retirement or have some type of ownership or financial incentive to stay on with their current employer.

What did candidates tell LinkedIn were the reasons they don't want your job? The number one reason was they didn't know what your culture or work environment was like. Basically, they couldn't tell from your talent attraction strategy what it was like to work at your company.

Back to basic human psychology. I have a job. It may not be great, but I know what I know. I could change and take your job, and it may be incredible, but it also may be awful. Almost all of us will keep what we know over the risk of leaving for something we don't know, even when we are unhappy in our current position.

This is the simplest reason to get your story in front of candidates in a format and at a time they want to consume it. Employment branding and recruitment marketing: you have a story. The best talent will not take your job if they don't feel they know your story. It's a fairly simple problem-solving exercise. Tell them your freaking story!

Job Advertising Works!

Employment branding professionals and recruitment marketing professionals will always argue over what is more important. The brand or the advertising?

Over the years, what I've learned is that almost all of us have the same employment brand. We are all the "best place to work." We are all the "employer of choice" for our market. We all offer "great pay and benefits." It has all become noise to candidates. When I survey candidates about a specific employer within a market, usually, the vast majority of candidates can't even tell me what that employer does as a product or service! Most find out in the interview or in prepping for the interview. That is our reality. We all basically have the same employment brand.

The one difference I consistently see from employers who have less trouble hiring is they are better at job advertising. They simply run more effective job ads. They budget more money for job advertising on average than other employers in their market. More candidates know they have open jobs.

There is a classic real estate industry experiment that has been recreated time and again, based on determining who is the top real estate agent in your area. The experiment is quite simple. You go into a neighborhood or small town, and you survey a couple of thousand people, asking them, "Who is the Top Realty Agent in town?" The results are always similar. No one agent has a majority. Dozens of agents are listed, and the most any one agent has is in the teens as a percentage of the market.

The experimenter then does an eight-week ad blitz in the market. Each week, each house in the market gets a direct mail piece introducing the "top real estate agent" in the market. This person is completely fake. No one in the market has ever met or used this agent. For eight straight weeks, a new direct mail piece about this agent is sent to every home. The piece changes each week, but each piece is basically telling the homeowner this fake agent is the best in the market.

What do you think happens when the experimenter does the survey over after eight weeks?

Remember, prior to sending these ads, no single agent, real agents, actually selling houses in the market had captured more than around 15 percent of the vote when homeowners were asked who the top agent in the market was.

The fake agent gets over 60 percent of the vote when homeowners were asked about the top agent in the market! An agent no one had ever met, who had never sold a single house.

Advertising works because people trust what they are told in advertisements. We believe that someone can't just make up stuff and advertise it. "False Advertising" is against the law, right? It is for certain things. For instance, you can't say that a certain medicine will cure a disease that it can't. But, you can call yourself the number one employer in your city in a job advertisement because it's your opinion, and you could argue it's the opinion of your employees if you were ever challenged. But you won't be.

Did you know less than 5 percent of employers ever fill out the best places to work application? So, when someone says, "We are a top 100 best place to work!" it's kind of like them saying, "We are the tallest of the seven dwarfs!" They are only really the best place to work for those whom they were compared to who also happen to be the only other people who filled out the application. But what about all the other employers who never filled out the data? This isn't an indictment on those best place's services. I actually believe organizations trying to achieve that status probably are better places to work, but it's not really what it seems.

If I'm given a lot of money to fix recruitment and have a short time to do it, I spend most of that money on job advertising because it works.

Here's the thing . . .

Candidates don't know who you are. No, they don't. We love to believe they know us, but they don't. Around 99.99 percent of organizations do not have a recognizable employment brand. That's reality. Don't overthink it. Candidates don't care. They see us all the same. This is why you have to aggressively advertise your jobs. Humans believe in advertising because we want to. Job advertising works. Even bad job advertising works. Yes, be a great place to work . . . blah . . . blah . . . blah. But advertise the hell out of your jobs.

» 11 «

Hire More Pretty People

What do you think of when I tell you someone is a "sexy blonde model type?" Do you think this person would be dumb or smart?

What about: "Strong athletic jock?"

What about: "Scrawny nerdy band geek?"

My guess is most people would answer: dumb, dumb, smart, or something to that extent.

In human resources (HR) we call this profiling, and make no mistake, profiling is done by almost all of our hiring managers. The problem is that everything we might have thought about the correlation between looks and smarts is probably wrong. So, why are ugly people smarter? Turns out, they're not!

Slate published an article that contradicts all of our ugly people are smarter myths and actually shows evidence to the contrary. From the article:

> Now there were two findings: First, scientists knew that it was possible to gauge someone's intelligence just by sizing him up; second, they knew that people tend to assume that beauty and brains go together. So, they asked the next question: Could it be that good-looking people really are more intelligent?
>
> Here the data were less clear, but several reviews of the literature have concluded that there is indeed a small, positive relationship between beauty and brains. Most recently, the evolutionary psychologist Satoshi Kanazawa pulled huge datasets from two sources—the National Child Development Study in

the United Kingdom (including 17,000 people born in 1958), and the National Longitudinal Study of Adolescent Health in the United States (including 21,000 people born around 1980)—both of which included ratings of physical attractiveness and scores on standard intelligence tests.

When Kanazawa analyzed the numbers, he found the two were related: In the U.K., for example, attractive children have an additional 12.4 points of IQ, on average. The relationship held even when he controlled for family background, race, and body size.[1, 2]

That's right HR pros, pretty people are smarter. I can hear hiring managers and creepy executives that only want "cute" secretaries laughing all over the world!

The premise is solid though! If you go back in our history and culture you see how this type of thing evolves:

1. Very smart guy gets a great job or starts a great company. (Before you go all woke on me, take a breath. We are talking historically and right or wrong, it was mostly men who worked jobs and started companies.) He makes a lot of money.
2. Because of this success, the "smart" guy now has many choices of very pretty women to pursue as a bride.
3. Smart guy and pretty bride start a family, which genetically has a greater chance of resulting in pretty, smart children.
4. Pretty, smart children grow up with all the opportunities that come from being born into smart, beautiful, successful families.
5. The cycle repeats.

Now this is a historical thing, thus my example of using a "smart guy" and not a "smart girl." I'm sure in today's world this premise has evolved yet again. But we are talking about how we got to this point, not where are we now. Additionally, we are looking at how your organization can hire better. So, how do you hire better? Hire more pretty people!

It's interesting that when I espouse this premise at cocktail parties and work dinners there is always a sub-group of people who find this entire concept of hiring pretty people offensive. Why are they offended? Most likely they consider themselves ugly. Which, honestly, makes me feel bad because I like to think pretty is a state of mind. I myself am a shorter white male ginger. Not the poster for pretty in most cultures. But, I have this weird tick called confidence where when I look in the mirror I see a pretty person! (Author's note: But when I see pictures of myself, I always wonder what happened to that pretty person in the mirror!)

There is also some research around this concept of pretty. Researchers at the University of Missouri and DePaul University found that one's own attractiveness is key to your life outlook.[3] From the research:

> Three studies examined the association between physical attractiveness and meaning in life. Study 1 (N = 305 college students) showed that self-reported physical attractiveness positively correlated with meaning in life. Study 2 (N = 598 non-college adults) replicated the association between self-reported physical attractiveness and meaning in life and extended those findings, demonstrating that outside perceptions of attractiveness are linked to outside perceptions of how meaningful a person's life is. Study 3 (N = 331 targets, 97 raters) replicated these findings and probed the nuances of the relationships between outside ratings and self-reports of attractiveness and meaning in life. Across the studies, existential significance, or the feeling that one's life matters was the facet of meaning that primarily explained the link between attractiveness and meaning in life. In addition, a person's view of their own attractiveness is more indicative of their well-being than outsider ratings. Implications for our understanding of meaning in life are discussed.

This also plays into the narrative that pretty people make better hires. We like to hire people who are also confident. If you believe you are pretty you will have a better outlook on your life, which includes your job.

If you've been in HR or talent acquisition for any length of time, heck, if you've been alive in the world, you've probably run into some organizations where you are struck by how pretty everyone is when you walk in. You think to yourself, what are the hiring criteria to work here?! Do you have to be beautiful?! Honestly, that probably happened because of some bad hiring bias, not scientific research and facts like I'm giving you. But, if you paid attention, was the company you walked into with all of those pretty employees successful? In all my years, I've never seen a company full of pretty people that wasn't successful! Now that's anecdotal research and not as factual, but it's my experience.

The reason we just don't stop everything we are doing to hire great quality talent and just hire pretty people is because it sounds dumb. It can't be true. I mean that would be like only hiring college athletes because we think they're more competitive than non-athletes. Or hiring Dungeons and Dragons players because we assume they're nerds and smart.

I know companies who test for IQ and will use the results of the IQ test as the primary measurement when making hires. It seems logical. Hire smart people. Even if they suck, at least you hired someone with the capacity to understand how to do the job. When you say, "I'm going to use 'pretty' as our main criteria," we immediately believe we are hiring dumb, and no one wants to hire dumb people.

I'll challenge you to test this theory, though. Put a pretty candidate and a not-as-attractive candidate in front of a hiring manager where the skill level is basically the same. Who do you think will get hired? Ugly people know this bias. Every single time, the pretty person gets hired. We equate "pretty" with competent and "ugly" with, "Why can't this person make themselves more pretty?" Even when the hiring manager is ugly, they'll always hire the pretty person. I tell entry-level candidates and new graduates all the time, you might not be "pretty" but make yourself as pretty as you can be when you interview, it will make a difference to those selecting. That is popular HR talk. That's real talk. I backed it up with science!

Here's the thing . . .

We make all kinds of dumb hiring mistakes. "We only hire from Ivy leagues schools," "We only hire people with degrees." Is hiring only pretty people any different? Bias is bias. Every hiring process has bias. They key is knowing what your bias is.

» 12 «

That Which Gets Measured, Happens!

"The metrics to running HR are already in the business. You don't need to create new ones!"
— Patty McCord, former CHRO of Netflix

I heard Patty McCord speak at Saba's annual customer conference in 2017.[1] Patty was the first HR leader at Netflix before the company became crazy successful like it is now. Remember getting DVDs in the mail from Netflix and sending them back? That's when McCord was in charge, and she helped grow it into the organization it is now.

McCord believes that we in human resources (HR) and talent acquisition (TA) have a problem in that we keep trying to come up with new metrics in our function when instead we should just focus on how we affect the business measures already in place. How does TA help increase margins? Or top line sales? Or reduce overall expenses?

I love the concept because I think the more we can tie our function success to business success, the more valuable we become to the organization as a whole.

As a leader in talent acquisition, the only thing that will ultimately matter to your executive team will be your results. Great, you hired and trained a great group of recruiters. You built the perfect TA tech stack to attract talent to your organization, and you're winning awards for your employment branding and candidate experience. None of that matters if you don't have the bottom line TA results of quality hires in a timely manner for a cost that doesn't break the bank.

Measuring success in talent acquisition may be the most controversial and misunderstood area in all of talent acquisition. Part of this has to do with no one liking to be held accountable, so when it comes time to build metrics and measurements we tend to give ourselves enough room so that even if we aren't successful, we can still "look" successful.

The most widely used talent acquisition metric around the world, time-to-fill, is also the most useless metric to judge talent acquisition success ever created. I won't say it's completely worthless, but it's pretty close to worthless. If you're measuring your recruiting team's success by telling your executives you reduced your time-to-fill by 6 percent last year, you should be looking for a new career.

Why? Time-to-fill (TTF) doesn't actually measure the success of recruiting, and there are way too many variables at play to tie back success or failure to any one thing. Plus, if I truly care about my recruiters and their performance, I wouldn't use a measure they have so little control over the outcome of.

What TTF really does is measure the length of your recruiting process. The problem is, your recruiters may only control around 40 percent of that process. The hiring managers control a good portion, along with others who get their hands in the process for various reasons. Would you want to be measured on something where you don't even control half of the outcome?

Your recruiters find great talent and send it to a hiring manager, who then sits on the résumé/application for two weeks. Finally, they give your team some feedback and want to set interviews, which may take another seven to ten days. They interview and then sit on their decision for more days. Each of those segments adds to the total TTF, and your team, besides hounding the manager, really has little they can do to move the process further.

The other issue with TTF is that most organizations are dealing with dozens, if not hundreds, of different positions they're trying to fill. An entry-level service job in your organization may take you less than a day to fill. Highly specialized science-related positions may take you months to fill. In one period, you may have a lot of easy fills and hardly any hard fills, and your metrics look outstanding. Are you truly outstanding for that period?

So, we know that TTF as a measure of recruiting success is filled with issues. One TA leader I know, Jim D'Amico, talent acquisition leader at Celanese Corporation in Dallas, TX, worked at a previous organization where executive leadership used time-to-fill as a measure of TA.

Knowing all the issues with TTF, Jim set out to deliver a metric that measured every single part of the process by process owner. So, while your true time-to-fill measure on any one position may be forty-five days, those forty-five days are actually owned by different parts of your organization. Digging into those days owner by owner is critical to understanding how you would actually improve this measure.

Jim and his team would track—first via spreadsheets, eventually by business intelligence software—the entire talent acquisition process from approval of a requisition to start date for each position. Requisition approval is owned by someone. Then he would measure how long it took from the point the hiring manager got approval to hire to the next step. Maybe in your process that next step would be posting the job or sourcing candidates.

Recruiting would own that part of the process and the clock was ticking. Once a predetermined number of candidates were sourced, screened, and sent to the hiring manager, the clock stopped for recruiting and started for the hiring manager. The hiring manager would look at the candidates, give feedback, and determine which ones to interview. The clock stopped for the hiring manager and then it was on to the next step in the process. You can figure out the rest based on your process.

Now, your executive team and all the stakeholders of the recruiting process know exactly what's going on and who is responsible for what bottlenecks. With this information, you can work as a team to try and figure out how to eliminate bottlenecks within your process to make it faster, assuming you've determined that not getting candidates fast enough is the issue.

When I consult with TA leaders and they bring up TTF as a measure that needs to improve, I'll ask them, "Why?" or, "How do you know this measure needs to improve?"

The answer to this is important. If there's a business reason why you need to hire faster (for example, we can't get projects completed on time and we're losing money), then, by all means, let's dig into this and solve it. If the answer is, "Well hiring faster is always better," I have to stop them because faster does not equal better. Faster equals faster.

In talent acquisition, if your goal is to hire the best talent, faster does not help you hire better. There is a sweet spot for every organization and every position where waiting longer to find a "better" candidate probably has diminishing returns, but moving too fast also puts you in a position where you don't get to see the majority of the talent available within a market.

The entire reason TTF was created to measure success of talent acquisition was because hiring managers were frustrated with how long it took their recruiting teams to find them talent. We've already talked about this in an earlier chapter: if your organization is solely relying on you to produce talent, then you've already failed. If you're being forced to measure time-to-fill, at the very least, you need to add in some hiring manager accountability.

Okay, Smarty. What Should We Be Measuring in Talent Acquisition?

When I look at measuring success within a talent acquisition function, there are really two components:

- Individual recruiter success.
- Overall talent acquisition success as a function.

Most organizations work to try and measure their overall talent acquisition functional success but shy away from individual recruiter success. If I'm leading a talent acquisition team of three or thirty or three hundred recruiters, I need to know which ones are having success and which ones are not. Most TA leaders have no idea which recruiters on their team are truly performing over those who aren't. We have a lot of "feels," but not much more than that.

Recruiting and sourcing are activity-based professions. If you have recruiters on your team telling you differently, you now have a list of the first people you need to get rid of. Look at the classic graph of any talent acquisition function in figure 12–1.[2]

Figure 12–1. Talent Acquisition Funnel

You've seen a thousand of these funnels if you've been in talent acquisition for any amount of time. Talent acquisition stole this from sales. It's a basic sales funnel. Why did we steal it? Because it fits perfectly into what we do. Talent acquisition at its core is a sales function.

We have something to sell; in fact, we have two things to sell. We are selling our organization, and we are selling specific opportunities we have within the organization. Someone might love your company, but hate the job you have open. Or they might love the job, but not think too highly of your organization.

Every recruiter is constantly doing this double sell. In corporate talent acquisition, we get confused with this concept of TA as sales. We believe, far too often, that candidates should be selling themselves to us. The problem is that this is a broken concept.

You might argue this is really just a function of economic timing. In great economic times and low unemployment, we sell ourselves to candidates. In bad economic times and high unemployment, candidates sell themselves to us. I would argue that no matter the unemployment rate, we in talent acquisition always have to be selling our organizations and opportunities because of one simple fact: great talent doesn't have to sell itself.

If you are truly trying to hire the best talent in your market, you must sell what you have. Way too many talent acquisition organizations are overly conceited, believing they have the power, and the candidates should be bowing down to them and their almighty jobs. In the real world, this isn't the case. If you are one of these organizations that believes you have the power, you're not even coming close to the best candidates, because the best talent doesn't put up with that nonsense.

So, talent acquisition is an activity-based, sales function. If that is the case, we know from successful sales organizations that those sales professionals who do more of the right sales activities are more likely to have higher success than those who don't. Pretty simple concept, but no matter the industry, it always plays out in a similar way.

There is no difference in talent acquisition. For over twenty years, I've been measuring recruiter activity in both corporate and agency recruiting teams, and 99 percent of the time, those recruiters who have the highest level of activity will be the most successful. Also, the less experienced the recruiter, the more activity they need to find the same success as an experienced recruiter, so as leaders, we need to ramp up the activity levels of our newer recruiters.

In my recruiting shops, I measure everything in the funnel: phone calls (both incoming and outgoing), initial pre-screen interviews of candidates, the number of screened candidates who were passed on to hiring managers, the number of interviews of those candidates that were passed on, the number of offers made from those interviews, and so on.

It's like the recruiting funnel above, exactly. Having these measurements allow us, as TA leaders, to effectively determine the resources we need to do the job our organization is asking. If you know it takes a hundred candidates interested in a position to ultimately get one great hire, and the organization comes and says, "Hey, we will need to hire a hundred more in the next three months," you will be able to tell them exactly how many resources you need to get the job done.

That's ten thousand candidates into the funnel. That's a lot of sourcing and recruitment marketing that needs to take place. Then you need to screen a lot of candidates and set up all those interviews. If you have been tracking individual recruiter metrics on your team, you can accurately estimate if your team has the capability to accomplish this task, or how many more resources you will need to accomplish the project successfully.

If you have no idea what your recruiters are doing, specifically, all of this is just one big guess. We don't measure individual recruiter activity as a sole function of performance management. Measuring individual recruiter performance is also about resource management within the organization, and it allows you to specifically direct development to each recruiter as they need it.

You may have a recruiter who is the best at screening and passing on qualified candidates to hiring managers, but their ratio of screens-to-interviews is the lowest on the team. Right away you will be able to tell that development is needed on their screens because while they're getting the quantity, they're missing out on the quality aspect. You can then help them get better at this portion of the job and help them be successful.

Individual recruiter measurement is not about micromanagement; it is about helping your recruiters be the best they can be.

The first time I ever started tracking phone calls as an individual measure of recruiter success, I had no idea what to expect. I knew a recruiter had the capability of making 150–200 calls per week, outgoing, to candidates. What I didn't know was how much time a recruiter would spend on the phone, and when the first stats came back I was shocked at the number!

Do you know how long your recruiters spend on the phone each week? When I ask this question to groups of TA leaders, the answers usually range from twenty to thirty hours per week. Sometimes I even have a leader tell me forty hours! The first time I measured call volume and time, I didn't tell my team I had implemented the software. Not because I wanted a "gotcha," but because I wanted a true baseline of what was really being done.

The first month came back and the average call volume for a team of twelve recruiters was right around five hours per week on the phone. Five! My best recruiter spent around eight hours, and to be honest, all the recruiters on the team were very effective in their roles. Most TA leaders find this statistic shocking. But when you drill down and think about the role of a recruiter and how they make those 150–200 calls per week, you find most of those calls are just a few seconds of leaving a message.

Now, the five hours per week is combined incoming and outgoing call time. The 150–200 calls are only outgoing, and those ranges change depending on the incoming call volume and time. One week, a recruiter might make 200 outgoing calls but not get many incoming. The next week all those candidates call back, so their outgoing volume will be down, but their overall time on the phone will be higher.

If I have a recruiter who is struggling to get interviews, I can almost always go directly to his call volume in recent weeks, which will be lower than average, and show him why. Recruiting isn't hard if you put in the activity required.

So, I'll tell you right now, some will read this and think, "Oh boy, that's old school!" Remember, I'm measuring everything. The example above is phone calls, but I'll also measure text messages, emails, LinkedIn InMails, and so on. Of all those measures, the only thing that comes close to phone calls might be text messages for initial outreach. But, somewhere along the process for most positions we recruit, a phone call has to be made.

Would you accept a position, or take an interview for a position, without ever talking to a real person from the company? Ask yourself that question. Then, tell me whether or not phone calls to candidates matter. I will tell you, the better the talent, the more this matters. If you suck and are begging for a job, sure you'll accept an interview over a text message or email. If you're really good and highly sought-after, you'll never accept an interview over email. Never!

Many TA leaders, on the corporate side, are now beginning to measure "conversations," which are defined in a number of ways. You might have a text conversation with a candidate who would never respond to email, and would prefer not to have that conversation during work over the phone. Greg Savage, principle at the Savage Truth in Sydney, Australia, lays this out in three KPIs (key performance indicators) for a modern recruiter:[3]

- **Catchment.** A measure of how well your recruiters are building a talent community or network. If they're using LinkedIn as a tool, what is their weekly goal in growing their connections?
- **Conversations.** It may be a phone call, but it may be a combination of phone, text, email, Facebook messages, and so on. Are

your recruiters having conversations that lead to positive measurable outcomes?

- **Conversion.** From their growing network and conversations, how many of these things are leading to an actual conversion of an interview, someone to nurture for a future position, hires, and so on?

As TA leaders, we kid ourselves into believing individual recruiter activity isn't important, that our teams are adults and adults don't want to be tracked. This is why most corporate TA functions are failing in the world, this one simple concept of tracking individual success. It's simple performance management of an activity-based function. If you have recruiters who don't like this, you have people on your team who aren't really recruiters.

The Magical Holy Grail of TA Metrics: Quality of Hire

If I had one wish I could use to help out every single one of us who work in talent acquisition I would use that wish to create one overarching measure of quality of hire that every single organization in the world would use. Once we get past individual recruiter measures of success, quality of hire really is the next big thing our organizations need to determine TA functional success.

The problem is, none of us can agree on how quality of hire (QoH) should be measured. So many organizations measure quality of hire after ninety days, and then only measure the recruiting team against this measure. So, if a candidate leaves a position after ninety days, the recruiting team takes the hit and must have recruited a bad apple. Really?

The problem with QoH is that it's not fully a TA team measure of effectiveness. It is a great measure of the entire TA process effectiveness. Think about QoH and all that it would really take to measure the quality of each hire in your organization.

First, you need your recruiting team to find and screen good talent. Then you need a hiring manager to interview and make a great selection. Then you need to measure the performance over an extended period of time (probably a year, at least) to know whether or not that the person hired has performed or not performed.

Rob McIntosh, principal advisor and founder at McIntosh & Co., says that industry model of QoH probably looks like this:

Quality of Hire (QoH) = (APR + AE + HMS + ER)/N

APR = average performance rating for new employees in first year

AE = employee performance as a % of achieves expectations of performance in the first year

HMS = annual hiring manager survey

ER = % of employee retention first year of employment

N = number of indicators used

Example:

(68% APR + 94% AE + 80% HMS + 90% ER)/4N

QoH = 83%

Organizations have taken this measure and tweaked it to add in their own organizational indicators of QoH, which is one of the reasons we don't have an industry standard for quality of hire. Instantly, you can see why this measure is problematic. It's complex with a lot of variables that take time to bring together, and even then, it becomes a bit nebulous for most organizations to use as a true measure of TA process success.

McIntosh believes he has a model for QoH that is much easier to measure and probably speaks to the actual performance of your TA process:

Number of candidates submitted to the business that they accept as a % (recruiter accountability)

+

Percentage of candidates employed (retention) in their first year of employment (business accountability)

Divided by these two data points.

Example:

Figure 12–2. Quality of Hire

I love the simplicity of this measure of QoH, but also how it holds both the TA team and the hiring manager accountable to the measure. The TA team is held accountable for finding high-quality talent that the managers want to hire. The hiring managers are held accountable for retention. If a candidate is a bad hire, then it's up to the hiring manager to weed them out.

The reality is that the TA team has little to do with first-year performance. That is mostly a function of employee performance, hiring manager expectations, development, culture, and so on. So, placing a QoH metric as a sole measure of TA team effectiveness is worthless, but the actual measure of QoH is important to the overall measure of process success.

If you really want to have a "quality" metric in your TA measures, you should be using Quality of Applicant (QoA). QoA is the ratio of candidates you send on to a hiring manager to those who receive a request to interview.

Now, there are two things to consider when you measure QoA:

1. Are these applicants being sent to a hiring manager screened or just sent from apply?
2. Your benchmark should be 90 percent or more.

Yes, that means if your recruiters are doing their job, nine out of ten applicants should get an interview request from the hiring manager. We should assume the recruiter did the correct intake with the hiring manager, they know produced a great job posting, they sourced, and they did proper screening and assessment. If all that was done and they made the decision to send the applicant to the hiring manager, it should almost be automatic that an interview will be requested.

In fact, the best recruiters will negotiate this up front with the hiring manager. If I find someone I think is worthy of sending you, I need you to trust me, and I'm going to set up an interview on the spot when I find them. I say 90 percent because I'm not heartless! I mean, the hiring manager might have some knowledge of the candidate we don't have, so I'll give them one.

The problem is we've created an inefficient mess! We let our hiring managers believe we are just going to send you stacks of candidates, and you just let us know when you want more. No! We are wasting resources when we do this. I'm going to find you some amazing candidates for this job. I expect you'll interview all of them. If in those we don't find a great hire, we'll go back to the drawing board and figure out what we did wrong together.

The Real Magical Holy Grail of TA Metrics: Capacity Recruiting

Let's say your CEO walks into your office today and says, "We need to double our hiring next quarter!" What is your response? Over 90 percent of TA leaders at every size company, in every industry, will basically say something like, "Okay! We'll do it! We'll work 24/7 to make it happen!" The CEO will leave happy, but you truly have no idea what you just agreed to.

Capacity recruiting is knowing exactly what you can produce from a recruiting perspective. You know your capacity by measuring your recruiting funnel by the individual recruiter and by the team. Once you know your internal benchmarks, you will see by week and month what your team can actually produce. You will be able to see if you're at 90 percent capacity or 75 percent.

Then, when your CEO walks in and tells you to double your recruiting next quarter, you can have an honest business discussion about what is possible and what isn't. That discussion looks like this, "Awesome! I'm excited we are growing! We are currently at 90 percent capacity for recruiting. In the 10 percent extra capacity, I can give you another one hundred hires next quarter. To get to your double number, I'm going to need a few more, and those resources are . . ."

Because you measure your funnel, track your job advertising spend, and so on, you will be able to give your CEO an exact list of resources you'll need. No surprises. No, "Well, we worked super hard, but we just didn't get it done!" Working hard is not a strategy in talent acquisition. It's a road to ultimate failure. Our executives expect us to lead with data and understand the business. Capacity recruiting is using the language of business to effectively communicate with CEOs and CFOs who don't understand the business of recruiting.

Do Your Recruiters Make Hiring Decisions?

Few recruiters in organizations make actual hiring decisions. My hope is that as you become a talent advisor within your organization you would actually carry some pretty high influence into each of those individual decisions, but ultimately the decision to hire or not hire a candidate should fall onto the shoulders of that person who must direct the performance of that hire.

This is why measuring the success of talent acquisition is a tricky business. We are often judged on our performance based on how a hiring manager makes good or bad hiring decisions. Can you imagine a CFO of a hospital being judged on how well a nurse performs her duties? That is the same as saying a recruiter is good or bad at finding talent based on who a hiring manager chooses from a slate of candidates. There is very little correlation between the two.

Kris Dunn, CHRO of Kinetix and founder of the talent blog *Fistful of Talent*, loves to use the measure hiring manager batting average (HMBA) to help ensure that TA team success can be decoupled from decisions hiring managers too often make in a vacuum.

The formula for HMBA looks like this:

$$\frac{\text{All employees hired by a manager over a time period still with the company}}{\text{All employees hired by a manager over a time period still with the company + those employees who left over that same period of time}}$$

Usually, you need at least a year's worth of data to calculate HMBA. If you're lucky and you have hiring managers who have been in a position for a while, you might be able to get two or three years' worth of data.

The great thing about HMBA is you will instantly see your problem-child hiring managers who make bad hiring decisions. In baseball if you have a .300 or higher batting average you're an all-star! In hiring, if you have a .300 hiring batting average you should probably be fired!

I would look for most hiring managers in relativity low turnover functions to have an HMBA around .800–.900 or more. Most hiring managers should be able to make solid hiring decisions in 80 percent to 90 percent of their hires, or more. If it's a high-turnover function, you still look for hiring managers who can make a solid hiring decision at least half the time, or more.

Where this data comes in handy is when used at the executive level when discussing organizational turnover. Again, turnover and retention somehow become talent acquisition measures, when in reality, we have little control over whether an employee stays with the organization or not. A hiring manager, on the other hand, has a lot to do with whether that employee stays or goes.

Imagine your executive team looking at an entire organizational list of managers ranked by HMBA. What you see right off the bat is you have some managers who really know how to hire and retain. You also see some who are not so good. If you marry HMBA with manager department performance data, you will not be shocked that this usually plays out similarly.

Managers who have high turnover and low HMBA usually also have low business performance metrics across the board. Turns out, making great hiring decisions usually leads to great business performance.

This kind of data can be polarizing in an organization and should be handled with care. What I usually do is share this first with the hiring manager as a guide to help me open up the conversation about the importance of making good hiring decisions, especially with those I know are not making good decisions.

In a best-case scenario, I would partner up one of my hiring managers who has demonstrated being strong at making hiring decisions with one who has a low HMBA. I would have the one with a low HMBA go to interviews and watch the one with a high HMBA. I would have the one with a high HMBA sit in on interviews that those with a low HMBAs are having and then give the feedback after, privately. The goal is not to use this data as a hammer but to help hiring managers get better.

The last thing I want to do as a TA leader is to have to hire another person. Each person we retain as an organization is a positive to TA. Each hiring manager who makes a better hiring decision is a positive to TA. Each time I don't have to hire in TA is a win for TA.

Making It Rain in TA

Cost of hire is a typical TA measure within organizations. It makes sense: we want to know how much it will cost the organization each time we hire someone. Unfortunately, this metric is rarely used correctly, and as another metric that has some many outside influences, it becomes extremely hard to make it accurate.

I tend to believe this is also a metric that was made up by vendors so that they could prove ROI of the tools and services they sold us. "Okay, your cost of hire is $2,000, but you used our new magic wand and now it's only $1,900!" We must need more magic wands!

Most organizations only look at resources being spent to calculate cost of hire and leave out their largest cost, which is usually the headcount and benefits of the team. When looking at technology solutions, one big savings is always a reduction in hours needed, and thus headcount needed.

Also, cost of hire is measured in so many ways, it's truly hard to measure yours against other organizations' as a measure of comparison. It can, though, be used as an internal comparison over time, as long as you keep the variables within your measure consistent. We all want to run our TA operation as inexpensively as possible, given we can get the same level of success or better.

As leaders, we need to be careful when cost of hire as a metric becomes an overriding measure of success, and finance starts looking at it as an operational measure of success and starts asking for annual reductions in cost of hire. "Hey, last year our cost of hire was $2,000 per hire; next year we would like it to be 4 percent less." Yeah, and people in hell want ice in their water, but I can't make that happen either!

The reality is cost of hire moves with the unemployment rate, market competition influences, overall team experience, tech stackability, and so on. You might have a string of years where each year you drop your cost of hire, then in one year, you will see a 25 percent increase. That increase may have nothing to do with TA success but be totally market driven. This is one reason I do not like cost of hire as a metric of TA success.

Measures I do like TA leaders to use are source of hire and spend by source of hire. Source of hire simply measures where each of your hires ultimately came from. Most of us will have anywhere from ten to twenty different sources of hire.

Currently, most organizations will have these sources of hire in their top five:

- Employee referrals.
- Job boards (Indeed, Google for Hire, LinkedIn, CareerBuilder, etc.).
- Career site.
- College recruiting.
- Job fairs.
- Internal ATS database.
- Recruitment marketing promotions.

It's pretty easy to measure source of hire if you build this into a consistent step within your TA process. Source of hire can sometimes be hard to measure accurately because we try and automate it through our applicant tracking system (ATS), and many times this data may not be accurate.

You might have a candidate who originally saw your opening on CareerBuilder, but then went directly to your site and applied for the job. So, is the source your career site, or CareerBuilder? A candidate found your job on Indeed but then sent their résumé to a contact at your company on LinkedIn. Is that source Indeed, LinkedIn, or employee referral? It can get confusing.

By building a step into the process where you have a candidate decide from a drop-down menu within the application process to tell you where they first heard about this job works well. It also helps to add into your process a step where the recruiter also works to find out this data by asking the same question and putting it into your ATS. It's interesting to see these side by side: candidate-proclaimed source and recruiter-discovered source. They will mostly match up, but sometimes you'll find discrepancies between the two.

Source of hire doesn't need to be 100 percent perfect. If you can get into the high 90s, it will be good enough. What I really need source of hire for is to marry this data with the actual spend on recruiting tools.

What I normally find with source of hire rankings is that employee retention is ranked one or two as a top source, but the actual spend on employee retention programs/technology is way down the list; sometimes not even in the top ten ranked by spending. I will also find some job boards, like LinkedIn, that will be down on the list at number five or lower as source of hire, but be number one or two in terms of spend.

As a TA leader, I need to get these two items, source and spend, in line with each other, as closely as I can. If I want more employee referrals, then I need to spend more on those programs and technology. If a job board is not delivering, I need to go back and negotiate a contract that is closer to its relative value for what I'm getting.

The sign of a great TA function is one that has this alignment in check, and one that knows what its most valuable sources of hire are and is putting the appropriate amount of resources into each. If you really want to ramp up this data, go back to your quality of hire metrics and add this data into your process as well in terms of alignment.

Ultimately, I want my top source to be my top quality of hires, and I want to be spending the most of my resources to use that source as well as we can as an organization. This is not hard data to get and track, and every TA organization should be doing it.

Are You a Successful Talent Acquisition Leader?

If you measure everything, you measure nothing. I want to measure a few things, but I'm going to be maniacal in my approach to measuring those things. Many will say that hiring manager satisfaction is critical to TA success, but I find it to be a low predictor of actual success.

Many times, my worst-performing recruiters will have high hiring manager satisfaction. They don't do the job of a recruiter, but boy do they make those hiring managers feel extra important! I think hiring manager satisfaction can give you some insight on and indicators to something going wrong early on, but I'll often see many high performing TA functions not using it because they find better measures of success.

For me, those measures are the ones we've already laid out. I want recruiters who are performing the activities we've decided will lead to success. I want to hire the highest-quality employees I can. I then want to double down and make sure I'm using the tools that are bringing me those best hires.

When it comes to leadership success within talent acquisition, I tend to rely on direct executive feedback. If I know my measures are in place and strong, it still doesn't mean I'm being perceived as a strong performer as a TA leader.

I can't tell you how often great TA leaders, with really strong processes and technology and who are performing admirably, are let go by an executive team because they didn't do one simple thing: the TA leader never found out from the executives what success looked like from their vantage point.

Never discount the opinion of what success looks like to those in charge. Just because you have one vision of success does not mean that will be a shared vision. In fact, it's often easier to find out what talent acquisition success looks like up front from your executive team and line of business leaders, and then you can build your approach from this starting point.

Also, keep going back and level set with your executives that this view of success has stayed the same. We all change our minds over time. A year ago, I saw this as success, then you went out and killed it and became more successful than I thought you could. Now, I have a new vision of success for TA. Many times, we are a victim of our own success, but I'll take that!

Too often as TA leaders, we believe our measure of success is all about filling positions. If it was only about filling positions, talent acquisition would be easy, because filling positions might be the easiest thing we do in TA.

TA leader success is not about filling positions. It's about filling positions in the time we need them filled, at the cost we have available to fill them, with the talent level required to maintain and grow the success of the business. Far too often, all of these things are working against each other, which makes TA success difficult.

The designer's holy triangle states that you can have something fast, cheap, and good—you have to pick two:

Good + Fast = Expensive
Good + Cheap = Slow
Fast + Cheap = Inferior

In talent acquisition, we are asked to provide all three with no downfall. Our leaders want the best talent as fast as possible for the best possible salary. We can't be expensive, we can't be slow, and we can't hire inferior talent. The talent acquisition holy triangle of success is meeting all three without exception.

Here's the thing . . .

Recruiting is a sales and marketing game. You must measure your funnel for the simple fact you must know what your recruiting capacity is for your organization. If you do not know you're capacity, you are flying blind as a leader, and you look weak to the other functional peers you interact with. Measure the recruiting funnel by each individual recruiter and by the organization. It's the only way you'll know what is being done and what your recruiting capacity is. One last thing, if you're using any version of Time to Fill as a recruiting success measure, just know you should be fired.

The White Guy's Guide to Fixing Diversity Recruiting

Hi, my name is Tim Sackett, and I'm a white guy.

In our industry, that means I cannot solve or speak to anything related to diversity, equity, inclusion, and belonging (DEI&B).

End of chapter. (Author's note: I actually did my 23andMe DNA testing, and I'm not fully white! I'm .2 percent Native American. Suck it, haters! I'm First Nations!)

Okay, now that we have that out of the way, let me tell you what I would do.

Diversity Recruiting is a scam.

What we are saying by having things like "Diversity Recruiting" is saying we don't do "real" recruiting well enough, so we have to add another entire function to fix how bad you are at the original function!

Can you imagine your CFO announcing that they are going to start a new function called "Actual Accounting" because the accounting team is so awful at their jobs we have to supplement them with another department that can do actual accounting? No. It would never happen!

But somehow, in talent acquisition, we've failed to deliver an inclusive slate of talent to our hiring managers, and instead of fixing this problem, we've created an entirely different department that needs all the same resources as the actual recruiting team. And the most amazing part about this is no one has raised their hand in a board meeting and said, "Um, quick little question here. Why don't we just fix recruiting?"

For some reason, our recruiting teams are great at recruiting white men, white women, and probably some other ethnicities based on the type of hiring you do, but we just can't figure out how to hire people of color. Doesn't that seem really strange?

We don't need different recruiting departments. We need to fix the one recruiting department to deliver the full talent needs of the organization.

This goes for military recruiting as well.

Okay, smarty pants, how do we do that?

I told you, it's the other chapters of this book. TL;DR. Okay, here you go:

1. Hire recruiters that are diverse, like the populations you want to attract and hire. Want more women? Hire female recruiters. What more people of color? Hire people of color to recruit. What more military hires? Hire vets and teach them how to recruit.

2. Gather data around the demographics of candidates for each role you are hiring for. Why? Because you'll look stupid trying to hire 50 percent of your Software Engineers as black women when you are located in Duluth, Minnesota. You have to set realistic and accurate goals for hiring. The goal should never be "more." If 12 percent of the registered nurses in my market are men, I should have 12 percent of my nurses be men. If 17 percent are black women, I should have 17 percent that are black women if my organization wants our employees to represent the market we are servicing.

3. Fill your funnel with an inclusive slate of candidates. This takes great recruitment marketing, job advertising, employment branding, employee advocacy groups, and community outreach.

4. Measure the funnel and include gender and ethnicity in your measures. You should know what your mix of candidates is at every segment of your recruiting funnel so you can identify when and where your bias happened.

5. Stop the bias. No, really, stop the bias. Jim, the hiring manager, doesn't like to hire black folks. We know he doesn't because we can see in our data that he constantly rejects black folks. Go punch Jim in the throat. Don't allow Jim to hire any more. Build diversity hiring scorecards by hiring managers that are posted publicly.

6. Rinse. Repeat.

Hiring any certain type of candidate isn't hard. It's a focused process that is unrelenting.

This isn't a chicken or egg issue. Too many people in our industry will espouse that we first have to make our organizations welcoming to diverse candidates. No. You have actually to have diverse employees to make this happen. A bunch of one kind of employee can't comprehend how to build a diverse culture when there is no diversity.

Imagine a company of one hundred women. Now they want to add some men. But first, they believe they need to prepare the "culture" for these new male employees. Do you think we should make all the women watch action movies and read about sports? Doesn't that sound dumb? Yes. You would bring new male employees in, and you would have them help build this new culture. Is it going to be hard and evolve change? Yes. If it were easy, we wouldn't have failed at this for so long.

Diversity recruiting professionals will hate this. I understand. But we don't need more diversity recruiting. We need more good recruiting.

Here's the thing . . .

If you recruit the way you should be recruiting and measure what you should be measuring, you don't need any "specialized" recruiting. We feel we need diversity recruiting because we refuse to hold our recruiters and our hiring managers accountable to a desired standard. Because of this lack of accountability, we justify wasting the resources of the organization.

What Does the Future of Talent Acquisition Look Like?

R obots!
Just kidding—that would be an easy way to start a chapter on the future of talent acquisition (TA) because artificial intelligence (AI) is all the rage in recruiting. The reality is the future of talent acquisition *is* all about innovation, and that might be robots, or it might be balls of energy that haven't even been created yet. Who the hell really knows?

The problem with innovation is it's really difficult to predict which innovation will have the most positive impact on recruiting in your organization. We tend to be fairly conservative in corporate talent acquisition and human resources, and even more conservative when making decisions that impact what little budget we are given to actually run our shops.

In HR and TA, we tend to be laggards when it comes to technology adoption. You can see in figure 14–1 that the HR technology adoption curve is way more conservative than the normal consumer adoption curve for technology.[1] What this chart is saying is consumers are using the latest iPhone and HR is still using a Blackberry!

None of us wants to be the leader who spends 50 percent of our budget on recruiter holograms only to find out it was a colossal failure and you better start looking for your next gig. Instead, we tend to wait for others to try out stuff, work through the bugs, and then we'll jump on board after it's been showed to work. We call this best practice.

Figure 14–1. Consumer vs. HR Technology Adoption Curve

Like Jim Collins said in his book *Good to Great,* "Good is the enemy of great."[2] I'm saying, "Best practice is the enemy of innovation." Let me clarify a bit because I'm not saying using best practices is a bad thing. If your TA shop is not running well, getting to best practice may be the next logical step to getting you fixed and on the right path. But never let yourself believe that best practice is the same as innovation.

Being an innovative talent acquisition function is a hard place to get. You just don't wake up one day and say to your team, "Today, we're going to innovate!" It doesn't work like that. Innovation happens when you give your team the room and encouragement to go out and try new technology and discover new ways of doing things. These 'tests' will fail, but every once in a while, you'll hit a grand slam and find something that is groundbreaking in how you discover, attract and hire talent for your organization.

I'm a big fan of Matt Alder's podcast *Recruiting Future*.[3] Matt searches the world for great TA leaders and professionals who are doing really cool stuff and then he brings them on his podcast to discuss. One such guest was Kerstin Wagner, head of talent acquisition at Deutsche Bank in Munich, Germany.

Germany has an exceptionally difficult recruiting environment. Low unemployment, growing economy, and a low birthrate combine to make it very difficult for organizations in Germany to find the talent they need. Even German universities are offering students from other countries free tuition and boarding if they will sign on to work for each year of schooling they get.

Deutsche Bank was one of those organizations struggling to hire the talent it needed, so Wagner started a digital and social think tank around talent acquisition innovation within her global team at Deutsche Bank. She and her team come together roughly every six weeks to focus on how they can make talent acquisition within their company more innovative. No limits, no boundaries, and no hierarchies are allowed within the think tank.

Wagner's team members look at three main areas for innovation inspiration. First, they scour their own industry, talent acquisition, to understand what others are already testing and trying. Could some of those things be things they also should be testing? Next, they look outside their industry into other industries to see how others are attracting talent, what the trends are, what technology they are using, and so on.

It's worth pointing out that Deutsche Bank doesn't just look at trends within HR and TA, but also at the technology and trends of what marketing is doing to attract more customers, and it tries to understand if that is something to leverage.

The think tank will take all of this brainstorming and make decisions on what they should be testing, assign the project to an individual or group, and make sure they have the budget and time to build out what is needed to be tested.

Then, like everything we do in talent acquisition, they will measure the effectiveness of the test and make decisions on whether this is an innovation that needs to be further tested, doesn't have the impact to continue, or maybe should be rolled out across the enterprise.

Wagner's biggest piece of advice for fellow leaders is to be brave.

The future of talent acquisition won't be decided by talent acquisition technology and service vendors. The future of talent acquisition will be decided by those leaders who have the guts to try new things and discover something no one else has yet tried that has a great effect on their organization.

Artificial Intelligence in Talent Acquisition was Designed for One Reason

When we talk about artificial intelligence in recruiting we tend to focus on "bots." Chat bots seem to be taking over talent acquisition from a technological perspective, and it seems like every new and existing piece of technology we use is adding in some sort of bot.

When most of us hear the term "AI," we are immediately drawn into the movie world of robots that are smarter than us, stronger than us, and are going to take over our world as we know it. From *The Matrix* to *I, Robot*, Hollywood has filled our minds with these wonderful pictures of what AI may become.

In talent acquisition, AI is much less sexy than the ultra-sleek, shiny, even-keeled, somewhat funny robots of the movies. I love Sonny from Will Smith's famous movie *I, Robot*. When I first saw the movie over a decade ago, I couldn't wait to have my own Sonny. If only I had a Sonny, I could do anything!

Most talent acquisition AI is something you'll never see. It's smart technology that sits behind your processes and can do most of the tactical work your current recruiters do, but faster and more efficiently.

Right now, not in the future, artificial intelligence can take your current job opening and source for candidates. It will then take those sourced candidates and rank them based on algorithms that will continue to get smarter the more you hire because of machine learning, about which of those sourced candidates will most likely be the most desirable for you to hire.

From the rankings, the AI will then reach out to these candidates and discover which ones are interested in your job and your company. From there, the bot will set up an interview with your hiring manager and send the candidate all the information needed. The first time the candidate will have contact with a real person from your company will be when she shows up for the interview—that is, unless you also use artificial intelligence leaders!

That's not the future. That is today!

The AI that will have the most effect on recruiting in the future is not bots, it's technology that you cannot see or touch. These artificial intelligence systems will invisibly go out and find your candidates, rank those candidates, and reach out and nurture those candidates, all behind the scenes, buried within your excising TA tech stack.

The AI that will take a recruiter's job will not be a robot, but intelligent automation that will begin to learn on its own and get smarter about the talent that performs best in your environment based on the success and failures of past hires you've made. Artificial intelligence will work throughout your full HR tech stack to predict and prescribe better people practices across the organization.

This isn't flying car kind of technology. We are very close to being able to embed AI in all of our TA processes and make us more efficient, less error prone, and much more cost-effective.

So, let's not kid ourselves about why artificial intelligence was developed in talent acquisition. The marketing for AI 1.0 in talent acquisition has been, "AI won't replace recruiters; AI will help recruiters!" Yeah, AI will help recruiters pack up their desks!

I know why marketing says this. If recruiters feel AI will replace them, they will be hesitant to work with it to make it work. Also, recruiters won't recommend and champion this kind of technology. So, instead, we tell them how great it will make recruiter's lives. "Now you can do all those things you haven't been able to do."

Like what? What are recruiters not able to do that they will now that they have all this time? Develop talent pipelines? AI will do that. Source more? AI will do that. Do better quality interviews? Okay, maybe, but only until AI learns that.

I am not an AI hater—I'm a huge fan. As TA leaders, we cannot be naïve to the reality of how a level of automation will affect our teams. If you need to hire more recruiters and sourcers, AI may be able to make that less of an issue. If you are all set, this technology is based on a return on investment that will lower your headcount. That's just a fact of how this equation works out.

AI in talent acquisition was designed to eliminate tactical work done by humans that can be done more efficiently, more productively, and with higher quality by these self-learning intelligent systems. That's a good thing in terms of the overall benefit to the organization. It will leave some bodies in its wake.

It's our job as leaders to reskill, find other sources of value that hiring managers need, and find ways to leverage AI for our benefit. Talent acquisition isn't the only function facing this new reality—so is every other function in your organization. The value of tactical work just became very inexpensive.

There Are Thirty-One Hours in a Day

One huge value of all this intelligent automation and artificial intelligence is the technology increases our overall time. All this technology allows us to multitask in a way we have never been able to in history.

The image in figure 14–2 shows us where we'll get our thirty-one hours and most likely what we'll spend doing those hours.[4] You'll notice that your daily work time is around five hours, because this is based on a seven-day week. It also means, though, that we tend to do a lot of non-work activities while we work, through multitasking.

Think about the amount of time at the office that you check into your social media accounts, listen to your streaming music service, pay a bill online, send a quick reply to a personal email, and so on. While this is the future of the work environment for us all, we also know from these behaviors how we recruit talent will also adjust.

One major bucket of time is video. The amount of video we all consume on daily basis is a little scary. We are constantly bombarded by video on our devices, walking down the street, sitting on the train, in a cab or Uber, in our offices, and so on. This level of video consumption is not going to stop anytime soon, and it's estimated to increase.

American Time Use Survey   AVERAGE HOURS PER DAY IN 2022

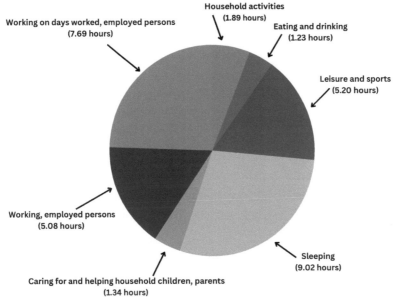

Figure 14–2. Average Daily Activity per Adult
Source: U.S. Bureau of Labor, 2022

Within talent acquisition, we will then have to adjust our strategies and tactics to match this appetite. Candidates do not want to take three minutes to read your job description. They would much rather watch a short video of your hiring manager telling them what the job is and what they are looking for in their next hire. That same candidate doesn't want to read Glassdoor reviews of your company; they would much rather watch current employees share what your work environment is like in a transparent way.

Most talent acquisition shops haven't even scratched the surface of video in employment branding, recruitment marketing, and every other part of your hiring process. Kansas City Children's Hospital uses HireVue to video interview potential candidates. That's not too awfully unique, as many companies are now using video interview technology.

What Kansas City Children's Hospital does differently is to have its patients, the children, also go on video and ask those same candidates the questions. Instead of the candidate reading the question, they now watch a short video of a sick child, the customer they will eventually work for, ask them questions like, "Why should we choose you to take care of us?"

That's a supremely powerful way to highlight your brand and culture. Kansas City Children's Hospital isn't Google; it isn't a unicorn (although they probably have some unicorns painted on the walls in the hallways!). They don't have buckets of money just sitting around. Their biggest resource was sick kids, but they found a way to leverage what they had to find the best talent!

One of the largest issues with video and organizations is that we (organizational leadership and mostly marketing) go a little crazy about video production quality. It may be that the biggest reason organizations never really leverage video is the cost of high-quality, highly produced final product.

We lose our minds over production quality. In reality, every kid in America is watching five-plus hours of video a day of some other kid on YouTube who is talking about what shows they're watching on Netflix and what they ate at school lunch.

You can produce good quality video in your own TA shop using a smartphone, an inexpensive microphone, and some cheap lighting. If you think you can't, there are more and more tech companies coming into our space that are doing this rather inexpensively as well.

One of those companies is SkillScout in Chicago, which will send you a video kit in a box and teach you how to make your own employment videos, and then they will do all the postproduction for you. What I love about organizations like SkillScout is they put small- and medium-sized businesses on an equal footing with our large company peers.

Our "fans" expect, or at least they will expect, video. Every single organization has fans. You don't have to be a unicorn organization to have people who love working for you, loved working for you, or would love to work for you! Every organization has at least one fan, or they wouldn't be in business. The future success of talent acquisition is about finding who these fans are, and then how you leverage that super-fan power.

We already know that for most of us, employee referrals are going to be our number-one source of hire. That won't change in the future. What will change is how we engage and nurture our fans. On average, about 50 percent of your employees will refer at least one candidate during their tenure with your organization, and about 30 percent will have referred multiple.[5]

If you add in alumni employees who were your top referrers, and any others outside the organization with the same behavior, and you capture all of these fans, you now have an on-demand referral engine at your fingertips. The power of this fan engine is that these people know your culture, love your culture, and they refer people who they believe will most likely be a better fit.

The technology is already in place with CRM and recruitment marketing platforms to capture this group, but very few are thinking in terms of fans. We still think linearly in terms of a job opening and filling that job opening. In the future, we will start seeing organizations worry less about filling specific jobs and focus more on finding great talent that wants to work at their organization, then creating the opening that best fits what the organization needs.

We already know that most of our jobs can be taught fairly easily, regardless of the education and experience a candidate is bringing with them. Thus, cultural fit, in the majority of occupations, becomes paramount to an organization's success. Your fans, internally and externally, are great judges of talent that will fit your culture. We just have to get better at letting our fans help us.

Your Future Talent Acquisition Function Will Have a Throttle

You know what a "throttle" is, right? It's a mechanism that, when engaged, makes a machine or your car go faster. If you push the throttle one way, the car goes faster; if you release the throttle, the car will slow down, or at least stop increasing in speed. One major problem with talent acquisition as a function is we don't have a throttle.

This works fine when hiring is slow, although we waste a ton of resources. It doesn't work at all when we hit times of high volume or increased hiring. Our throttle tends to be us working harder! Working harder is not a throttle, because it's hard to maintain over a long period of time.

In talent acquisition, if we want to increase our ability to place more people, we have few options. We can hire more people on our team. This is the number-one way we increase our capacity. We can increase our technology, which is usually our next option. We can also get outside help from staffing agencies, contract recruiting support, or recruitment process outsourcing (RPO).

In the future, TA will have a throttle that will work more like the gas pedal of your car: no need to increase your physical TA team, no need to add more technology, and no need to engage third parties. Talent acquisition technology is close to being able to deliver this throttle right now, and as artificial intelligence continues to get built into more of our systems, this is a reality we should be able to see very soon.

With the right TA stack setup, you should be able to post positions, have your tech source for those openings, screen those viable candidates, assess their skills, schedule interviews, and eventually even select, if you're comfortable enough to allow that to happen.

The throttle part comes in when you can also let your system know that in ninety days we will need to hire a hundred customer service reps for a large project. The technology will understand this bubble of work, understand when and how it will go about sourcing and nurturing candidates for these openings, and it will go to work filling your funnel at the appropriate time, with the appropriate numbers needed.

Sounds like flying cars and pipe dreams, doesn't it?

Right now, most of us are either understaffed or overstaffed in TA. I know, most of us believe we are understaffed, and there is a good reason for this. TA is usually understaffed because of this lack of throttle. Your chief financial officer is not going to have recruiters sitting around doing nothing, waiting for the next bubble of hiring to happen. This is also why we fail so often in talent acquisition: because we are not appropriately staffed and prepared for these bubbles.

Imagine the amount of waste an organization has when we have too many recruiters not hiring anyone. You would hope we would always be prepared with pipelines of talent just waiting for hiring, but that also doesn't work very well. Recruiters are not the biggest fans of engaging with candidates when they have nothing to offer them, so even our magical pipelines-of-talent models usually fail.

The proper way to handle this issue is to have a mechanism that allows your team to have the capacity available when it's needed. For my money, this is where artificial intelligence, chat bots, and intelligent automation will really add value to talent acquisition. I don't need AI to replace recruiters; I need AI to step in and allow me to throttle up my function when necessary, and then throttle down when it's not needed, while my core TA team continues to do the great work they were hired to do on a daily basis.

This concept of a throttle in business is nothing new. We see this in operations, accounting, and sales all the time. Every single industry has certain times when the workload is increased, and we all need the ability to meet those needs. Talent acquisition has traditionally used outside agencies to do this, at great cost, and far too often has become reliant on third parties.

I always look at third-party dependency as a misalignment of resources. If I need help to find some talent for my organization, and I don't have the capacity at this moment, then great, let's engage a third-party partner. If I'm engaging that partner every week and every month, then I have a core team issue that needs to be addressed.

The consistency of your third-party spend will tell you if you have capacity problems or core staff problems. Then, it's up to you to decide how to fix those problems. I'm in the business of selling contract staffing services, so believe me when I say that too many of us are not addressing our core capacity issues through proper staffing or proper technology.

While we're here, let's talk about who is actually in your "barn." It's traditional for TA only to be concerned with the actual full- and part-time employees it is responsible for hiring. Future talent acquisition shops will have their arms around everyone that is in their organization.

Modern organizations have a mix of full- and part-time employees, temporary employees, contract employees, consultants, virtual employees, onsite project staff, and so on. It's my barn, and I want to know every single person in my barn.

Why? Because of every single one of those kinds of people affects talent acquisition. Awesome, Mrs. Hiring Manager, you brought on a contract employee to help with our big business-transformation project. How long will they be here? Twelve months? Thirty-six months? A lifetime?

Organizations that hire contract employees for five-plus years while the average tenure of their employees is four years have a talent acquisition shop that has failed its hiring managers. A contractor for a certain period is fine. A contractor for life is a TA failure.

Using temporary employees to handle bubbles of work is normal. Using temporary employees on an ongoing basis because we don't know how to hire efficiently is a talent acquisition failure.

Also, when a hiring manager spends two to three times the average salary of an employee for short-term projects and uses an outside company to fill these positions with contractors for years and years, that is a talent acquisition failure.

Both of these things are happening in our organizations.

The future talent acquisition organization will track every single person in its barn, not just those who work for you. We will have systems to tell us when a contractor's assignment should be completed and will alert us when a hiring manager extends that assignment. It will alert us to all kinds of data and costs that are people related.

In TA, we need this information because it's all a measure of our failure or success. If IT is spending three million dollars a year on leveraging outside resources to get work done, we know as TA professionals, we should be able to find that same talent for a third of the cost if we could actually deliver. Can you imagine what you could do with all that money? Can you imagine the throttle mechanism you could build? The money is being spent; you just have to set up the process to know who's in your barn.

We Are All Unique, Special, Snowflakes! Our Moms Told Us So!

Marketing figured out long ago that consumers like to be treated specially. We like to be VIPs and first class and on secret, preferred lists. As consumers, we want things personalized to us; we don't want to be treated like one of the crowd.

Recruiting will become the same way. Your candidates do not want to be treated like all the other candidates. They want to believe you are only going after them, that they are "the one" you truly want to join the team. They want their experience to be personalized.

There are many stories of sports athletes being signed to one organization and then recruited to another when they become free agents. Organizations, in this moment, are just like you and me. They become recruiters at a whole other level to try and win the rights to sign these athletes to their teams. At a certain point, it stops being about money (because what's the real difference between $100 million and $101 million?) and it becomes about the basic need to be treated like they are wanted more in one place over another.

A great example of this was a number of years ago when a well-known professional basketball player became a free agent and traveled from team to team, hearing pitches about why he should sign with each. The story goes that the first team he got to had worked with an iPad app developer to personalize the iPad specifically for this free agent and team.

When the star arrived, the greeting committee handed the star the personalized iPad and showed him an itinerary of their time together, then told him it was his to keep.

The level of personalization that went into that first presentation definitely made an impact on the free agent and he ended up signing with them. Did a $500 device land a $100 million athlete? No, the personalization of a $500 device landed a $100 million athlete.

Whether we're making $100 or $100 million, we all want to be treated as if we are special and wanted. The basketball star told reporters that he felt like the organization that gave him the iPad showed they wanted him more. When pressed for details, he only gave the example of the iPad.

The future of talent acquisition is our ability to treat every single candidate like they are the only candidate. Right now, we could never deliver this kind of experience. Depending on your size, you would need to hire hundreds of people on your team to come close to being able to do this.

But, with advances in technology, we can see a future where every candidate gets the personalized attention and service they desire.

Many of us already have been able to deliver this level of personalization at the executive level, or with specific pockets of our hiring population. What if you could do this for that employee making ten dollars an hour? Can you imagine how powerful that would make your employment brand? Your organization would be able to pick the best of the best, because the best will want this level of personalization.

We already know younger generations entering the workforce will demand a higher touch, more personalized experience. Many organizations are working hard to figure this out, but it's mostly sweat equity at this point—manual processes that are hard to sustain and hard to scale.

Current technology that sends out personalized emails is also far from what any of us actually want. What we want is a feeling (that doesn't have to be reality) that the organization knows us, cares about our careers, and is attempting to match us to those needs. We want, at some point in the process, a real person who took more than twenty seconds to look at our résumé.

What we all want is an organization that wants us enough to put the time into making the experience of getting hired feel personal to who we are and what we want. The war for the best talent will not be won by who has the most money. The war for the best talent will be won by the organizations that can show they want them the most.

We Are the Netflix of Talent Acquisition

I always laugh at technology vendors when they say silly things like, "We're the Tinder for jobs!" or, "We're just like Instagram, but for job postings!" or, "You know Snapchat? That's us, but for talent!" We love to attach our product and brand to something that is infinitely more successful than ourselves because it makes us sound more successful than we really are.

I do think that most talent acquisition departments of the future can become the "Netflix of recruiting!" How? It's about streaming, baby! Pipelines of talent and talent communities are so early 2000s. Streaming talent, now that's so 2020!

How do you "stream" talent?

Talent streaming is a concept of hiring great talent when you find it, even if you don't have an opening, and then sticking that talent in a queue for when you want to watch—oops—deploy that talent.

Say what?

Here's an example of how talent streaming could work in your organization. Let's say you hire nurses. Nurses are hard to find. Experienced nurses in certain specialties are even harder to find.

One day, you are doing your recruiting thing and you find a sought-after specialty nurse, but you don't have a current opening for that nurse. Instead of just putting this nurse into some sort of a process or file for later, you contact that nurse to see if she would have interest in joining your team. It's your lucky day because that nurse wants to join your team. You give her the best candidate experience known to mankind. The nursing managers meet her and want to hire her. Everything else checks out, and the only thing left to do is make an offer and it's a done deal.

One problem, right? You don't have a freaking opening!

With talent streaming, you would offer this nurse a "conditional" position on your team. You would put her in "queue." She would be the next nurse to start in that department, as soon as an opening becomes available. Using your workforce plans, you can give her some insight to what that timetable may be. For this example, let's say it's within sixty days.

In the meantime, you will be paying this nurse to sit in "queue" while she continues to work at her current position. This amount is not a full-time nurse's salary but more like a consultant wage for a few hours per week. Let's say it's $100 per week to be in the queue or $800 for the sixty days.

During that time, the nurse would start doing a number of onboarding and training tasks, remotely and nonremotely. You would also sign an employment agreement that states certain assurances and protections for both sides. Of course, there would be some limits as well, but basically, all sides would have some skin in the game, and something to gain if the final outcome is met.

Here's the deal: we have the data to show when certain positions are more likely to become available, and these data are only getting better at predicting turnover. The real risk is not that we will never hire this person into a position; it's really that it might take a week or two longer than we expected.

Talent streaming is better than pipelining or talent communities because it's letting the candidates know they actually have something on the horizon given everything works out like it should. And with the properly signed agreement, both sides have outs and assurances to make everyone feel protected.

So, are you ready to start talent streaming?

This is the just-in-time kind of talent pipeline our hiring managers have been begging us to implement for decades. The problem with traditional pipelining is we haven't been willing to put skin in the game to show candidates we really do want them and have a place for them, but we just don't have the exact time, quite yet.

Putting off the start date seems like a small inconvenience in exchange for hiring great talent when we find it. Leaving some of these positions open for months on end costs the organization much more than the few hundred dollars it costs to keep a sought-after hire in the queue for your next position.

Yes, we just created the "Netflix of talent acquisition!" Oh, I'm sorry, Hiring Manager, did you say you wanted a *Stranger Things* account manager? Yep, we have that episode ready for download.

No one really knows what the future of talent acquisition will bring. Will it be robots? Will it be Netflix-style streaming talent services? Or will it be lots of people talking to lots of other people? Oh wait, wasn't that the past?

What we know is the future of TA will always be about leaders working with their teams and organizations to make the process more efficient for candidates, and presenting their organizations in the best possible light.

The future of TA will involve more automation and it will most likely take fewer people to accomplish more. By the way, this is the same future for every function in our organization and, as talent leaders, we need to be prepared and to prepare our teams for this reality.

The one thing that will never change in talent acquisition is our need and ability to attract the best talent we can to our organizations. That doesn't start with technology and automation; it ends there. Great talent attraction starts with great leadership vision and a story someone wants to be a part of. Happy hunting!

Here's the thing . . .

Talent acquisition, like every other function across the enterprise, will continue to be automated. We've only been doing this for over a century, so I'm confident that a century from now, we'll still be trying to make everything faster and more efficient. What we can't do is uncouple the human aspect of what we do in talent acquisition. Yes, robots and technology will make us better and faster, and even in some cases "more" human, ironically. But recruiting will always be a one-to-one human interaction at its core. The greatest TA shops will find out how to leverage great recruiting technology with great human interactions.

» 15 «

Talent Acquisition Advice from the Experts in Fun-Sized Chunks!

I like how the candy industry changed "bite size" to "fun size" in those big bags you get for Halloween. I like to think of myself as being "fun size"!

I've come to realize, after all of my years of blogging and speaking in our space, that my network has gotten pretty big. We've all heard of the game seven degrees of Kevin Bacon, where basically you make connections within seven degrees of the actor Kevin Bacon. Within the talent acquisition (TA) industry, I might be one or two degrees away from almost everyone in talent acquisition! That's not a brag. It's probably more just evidence to how long I've been putting myself out there on the social channels.

I get asked a lot by my network how they can help me, which is wonderful, but I rarely could find a reason to use them, until now! You read this entire book, basically getting my insight. Who knows, I might be totally wrong (I mean, I doubt that highly, but maybe). So, I decided to get a little help from my friends! Some of the top talent acquisition leaders in the world to give you their advice. The only thing I told them was no one wants to read your manifesto unless that manifesto is under 250 words! Give it to me in "fun-sized" chunks. Everyone loves fun-sized candy bars because you can eat like eight of them, and it doesn't count.

I hope you enjoy it and find great value in their advice.

Jim D'Amico, Talent Acquisition Leader, Holland America Group

Learn your company's business, particularly the mechanics of how they make money. Tie everything you and your team do into supporting that. If you can't tie something into that, don't prioritize it. TA doesn't exist to fill "jobs." We exist to increase share/stakeholder value. Filling jobs is one example of how we do that, but not the "Why."

Leading and managing are not the same thing. Leaders take risks and solve problems. Managers direct activity. Seats at the table are reserved for leaders.

D'Amico's Law: "Finding people is easy. Recruiting people is hard." (Author's Note: Jim totally stole this line from me!) Never confuse the two when designing strategy, selecting technology, or communicating to the CEO.

Never stop learning! Study TA practices and technology. Study the labor market. You will never be the trusted advisor to the C-Suite that you want to be if you are not an expert in your field.

Be an active part of the TA community. This is an amazing, sharing, and supportive community. You don't have to be an island. The community is there to help, always. I'm not the smartest TA Leader, but the people I know and ask for help are! (Author's Note: Jim is very smart because he understands this!)

Angela Shaw, SVP of Talent, Amplify Credit Union, 2022 Top Women Leader in Austin, TX

Include diversity, equity, and inclusion as a part of your talent acquisition strategy. Acknowledge that you will need to take a stand for it and prepare yourself by being knowledgeable about the subject matter. There is a famous quote, "Anything worth having is worth fighting for." I think about this quote whenever a conversation about diversity, equity, and inclusion is needed. Talent acquisition is always an impactful place to start, where you can diversify the makeup of your company using equitable practices that includes everyone. Are you doing that? Are you activating your power?

(Author's note: I 100 percent agree with Angela, TA is in the best position to impact DEI&B than any other function!)

Talent acquisition will always be one of the most powerful ways that a company can promote its commitment to diversity, equity, and inclusion. Every TA strategy should include it as a component with responsibility and accountability outlined. Most often, it is a conversation you will and must have across your organization in many ways and times. Recognizing this is a collaborative process with the people leaders and being action-oriented around the pushback needed to keep the organization on the path of its commitment to DEI is imperative. The world needs more of this fight from the people like you who have the power to push for change because we won't ever see the sustained movement towards the equity we all say we desire, and we do really need, without it.

Chris Hoyt, President, CareerXroads, former Talent Acquisition Leader at PepsiCo

Being successful includes not only matching skills to roles but also envisioning the future of talent within your organization.

Understand that technology will be your strongest ally. Embrace innovations like artificial intelligence (AI), machine learning (ML), and various automation within recruitment processes to streamline workflows and increase efficiency. These tools will assist in everything from applicant tracking to predictive analytics and robust people planning for future hiring trends. Understand the technologies available, find partners with validated claims on what they can deliver, and ensure your team is equipped to leverage those solutions effectively.

Prioritization is a non-negotiable skill for TA leaders. As you work to align the talent acquisition function with business objectives, remember that not all roles are created equal. Concentrate on strategic positions that will drive growth and culture. Consider the resources you have at your disposal outside of just budget; tech and data tools, industry networks and community, and continuing education/development. Use those resources wisely and know where to invest your time and energy.

As with any leadership role, managing change well within your organization is critical to success. Prepare your team for the inevitable. If we have been brutally reminded of anything over the last few years, it's that technology, industry norms, and the talent market are now hyper-fluid. This means that fostering an educated, resilient, and adaptable team and culture is key. Engage your team in open communication, provide ample training and development opportunities, and encourage them to embrace change. Involve them in the planning process, listen to their concerns, give them a stake in the outcome, and encourage internal mobility for their own growth whenever possible.

Finally, remember to measure success. Develop key performance indicators that are aligned with your business goals as well as those of your internal stakeholders where appropriate. Use these metrics to demonstrate your team's impact, drive continuous improvement, and communicate your successes throughout the organization. (Author's note: The vast majority of TA leaders don't do this well, Chris is right on point!)

Your vision, strategic thinking, and adaptability will be the cornerstone of your team's success. Be flexible, embrace inevitable change, and harness the power of technology to have an undeniable impact both within and outside of your organization.

Lotus Buckner, Chief People & Culture Officer, Chowbus

Align the business strategy with the candidate experience. Balance is key. It can be challenging to lead an enterprise talent acquisition function and balance the business requirements and an exceptional candidate experience simultaneously.

Get familiar with the company's business strategy, goals, and objectives, and align your TA strategies with these goals to ensure that you are impacting the business in a meaningful way. If the talent strategy is misaligned with the business strategy, it won't be sustainable.

Then, spend time truly understanding the target and potential candidates for the business—where they spend their time, what is attractive to them in a job, and what they care about. Develop your strategy in a way that connects things that are important to your candidates to things that are important to the business.

Some tangible things that can help accomplish this include building the right team and ensuring full transparency. Build and develop a TA team that understands how to find incredible talent using both traditional and creative avenues but also knows how to dive deep to gain a proper awareness of business needs. A strong TA team will have both great recruitment skills and business acumen. (Author's note: Transparency! I speak with so many CEOs who will tell me, "This is the first time I've heard this!")

Then, build in transparency as a core value to live by. The business should understand the market's expectations and trust your team's expertise on if and how to adjust their requirements. The candidates should clearly understand the process, timing, environment, requirements, and salary.

A winning team and strategy will consider both the business and the candidate's experience.

Christy Spilka, Vice President, Global Head of Talent Acquisition, iCIMS

The journey of TA leadership is exciting, always evolving, and incredibly impactful. One of the most important aspects of this role is how you lead your team. Empathy, communication, and a focus on development are important. Equally impactful is your say/do ratio (how often you do what you said you were going to do), your ability to remove roadblocks quickly, and that you always have their back. Over time, you'll sharpen your ability to balance your time effectively between the needs of the team, TA strategy, and company leadership.

Speed to trust across the organization is valuable, and TA has a lot of stakeholders. To build trust in your team, solicit regular feedback and ensure that you communicate early and often as you make changes or roll out new processes/technology. Always explain the why behind what you are doing. Maintain a focus on team engagement and recognize the accomplishments of team members regularly. Provide consistent coaching and annual TA training plans. When a roadblock is identified, work to remove it as quickly as you can. Be the voice of the accomplishments of your team and demonstrate your confidence in their ability. This will build the team's confidence. In your role, you'll have the opportunity to make a great impact on the business as well as on the people who will look to you for leadership.

Danielle Monaghan, VP Global Talent Acquisition, Google Cloud

Congratulations on the new opportunity! While it is exciting and energizing, you may be ready to implement all the new ideas and experiences you have gained over the years. My strong advice is to take some time to learn about the company's culture and what is valued before doing a 'cut and paste' of what worked for you at your previous company. Come in with a comprehensive listening and learning plan, and then create your 'doing' plan. Don't forget to talk to all stakeholders and vendors, including your frontline recruiting staff, RCs, candidates, new hires, the business, and all your people partners (business partner, DEI, ops, analytics, etc.) to ensure you have a deep understanding of what needs to be done, what the priorities are, and how much change management will need to take place. Once you have gained this knowledge and shared your findings and recommendations, be sure to do a thorough evaluation of the business strategy, the HR strategy, your team, and your leaders, processes, products, and technology, as these will be critical to the delivery of your TA strategy if they are right and if they are aligned. Then, together with your team, go make history!

Sara Bennett, Chief Talent Officer, Two Men and a Truck

My more than two decades of experience in the world of talent started in the most entry-level role the company had and took me to the C-suite, so I've experienced what it's like to work at all levels of a company. The best advice I have for people entering the world of TA is to never forget what the process is like for real people. We get caught up in data, trends, and new technologies and tend to forget about what it's like to be someone who is looking for a job or getting ready for their first day. Every now and then, take the time to fill out the application for one of your postings. Sit through orientation. If you're brave enough, have a recruiter interview you. Pay attention to what it feels like to be in the hot seat. Do your best to look at things through the lens of an applicant rather than through one of someone who is representing the company. Look for ways to eliminate roadblocks and frustrations in the application process. Find ways to share information in an engaging and useful way during the onboarding process. If you're not checking in with new hires regularly, make sure someone else is. Try to remember what an emotional process it is to put yourself out there as an applicant and how nerve-wracking it can be to step into a new company and a new role. We've all been that new applicant in our career journey; never forget to take the time to reflect and come back to what that new candidate experience is truly like.

Tracy Dodd, former Chief Talent Officer, Tiffany & Co. and Mastercard

I recommend that any new talent acquisition leader focus on strategy and experience. First, take time to listen to the business; talk to leaders and hiring managers, as well as HR business partners, to understand the hiring needs of the organization, now and in the future. Understand the strategy and how the talent needs may be shifting in the future. What skills are needed now and in the future?

Coupled with that, I recommend they also listen to recent new hires and candidates to truly understand the candidate experience. How are we communicating our employment brand? Are we living our core values throughout the recruitment process? Do candidates and new hires feel valued and welcome?

The TA strategy and candidate/new hire experience are jointly owned by the business. It is a partnership with many roles contributing toward a candidate and new hire experience that creates a strong talent pipeline, positive brand recognition, and employee success.

Kyle Lagunas, Head of Strategy, Aptitude Research, former Head of Talent Attraction, General Motors

Today's talent acquisition leader needs to know one thing: TA can either be the "Wild West" when it comes to the adoption of AI—with sourcers, marketers, and recruiters going rogue experimenting with new tools or exploring gen AI use cases—or it can be the "Field of Dreams," where everyone comes to play ball in the environment you've painstakingly built to support collaborative and controlled innovation. But there are no sidelines in AI; you're either winning or losing.

Whereas our colleagues across HR may be more focused on policing the proper use of AI within the world of work, you don't have that luxury. Talent acquisition professionals have always been faster to adopt the latest technology—anything that will make them more efficient and more impactful. This puts you in an awkward position: Do you support the drive to stay ahead of the competition and encourage folks to explore the possible, or do you err on the side of caution and limit the use of AI capabilities for the time being?

While you noodle on the best approach, consider that even your best efforts to limit the use of things like ChatGPT will not dissuade everyone. Many TA professionals like to solve problems and try new things—it's what keeps them on their A-game. And that's a good thing.

My advice? Find a balance—just like we did with social media and mobile. The rapid evolution of AI will arguably be one of the (if not the) most disruptive things in our lifetimes. You can't sit this one out. Now is the time to sit down with your talent ops and HR tech partners (and maybe your IT portfolio manager), and think about what a balanced approach looks like at your company. I guarantee your competitors in the market—the ones that are always attracting the best talent—are already a step ahead of you.

TL;DR—What was the advice from our expert TA leaders?

- Know your business before making changes. Even if you feel you know the business, the business has to see you getting to know the business. TA boots on the ground are never wasted time.
- Develop TA processes from the point of view of the candidate, not from your own point of view. Deliver an amazing candidate experience, and you'll have fewer recruiting problems.
- Align your TA strategy to the business strategy of your organization.

- Measure the things that truly measure your functional success, not measures that you can make look successful.
- People, process, and technology, in that order. Get the right people on your team. Develop a great hiring process that is candidate-focused. Implement technology that allows you to do all you do more efficiently.

Epilogue

People think it's a big deal when they find out you've published a book. And it is! Less than .01 percent of humans have a professionally published book. Around 2 percent of golfers can shoot under 80 for 18 holes. I now have two books and zero rounds of golf under 80. To a low handicap golfer, scoring under 80 seems easy, or at least doable. For me, writing, or at least ideas about what to write, comes easy to me. I believe that is the main barrier to why so few people have published books. I'm not sure why I have this skill, but here we are.

I think most people undervalue what they are good at. Thinking, "Well, if I can do it, anyone can do it." I wish more people would focus on what they are good at and get even better at that. Too often, we try to get better at something we like and ignore what we are already good at. You rarely get burned out at stuff you are really good at. I'm good at producing mediocre content in high volumes. So, more books to come.

I was never a writer. I was just a dude who liked to talk a lot and became a writer. That's why I write like I talk. Let's be professional and call it a conversational writing style. I envy real writers. I'm still amazed Ms. Kemp passed me in freshman English.

Shout out to very important people in my life:

1. Miss Kim—my University of Wyoming Hall of Fame wife. You don't write one book, let alone two, without much family sacrifice.
2. Kris Dunn—my best friend and the one who started this entire thing by getting me to start writing over a decade ago.

I had a lot of friends and peers contribute to this book, and I have a very large professional circle. My personal Board of Directors is two, Kim and Kris.

Thank you to everyone who helped me put this together and for all the community support. It takes a village.

Epilogue II

Is this ever going to stop?

If you have questions about anything you read in the book, just reach out to me. I'm easy to find. If you Google "Tim Sackett," I'm the first one hundred hits. There's also another "Tim Sackett" who is a truck driver chaplain. I'm not that dude.

Endnotes

Foreword

1.   Author's note: KD, I'm an equal opportunity hugger! I hug as many men as women! I hug you every time we see each other in person! In fact, the audience actually reacts better when I'm hugging a man. Unfortunately, we still live in a society where most audiences aren't comfortable with two men embracing on stage!

Chapter 1

1.   Andrew Perrin and Sara Atske, "7% of Americans don't use the internet. Who are they?" *Pew Research Center*, April 2, 2021, https://www.pewresearch.org/short-reads/2021/04/02/7-of-americans-dont-use-the-internet-who-are-they/.

2.   Bock, Laszlo, *Work Rules!: Insights from Inside Google That Will Transform How You Live and Lead* (New York: Twelve, 2015).

Chapter 2

1.   "Productive Aging and Work," The National Institute for Occupational Safety and Health, Centers for Disease Control and Prevention, last modified March 15, 2023, https://www.cdc.gov/niosh/topics/productiveaging/default.html.

2.   Richard Fry, "Millennials overtake Baby Boomers as America's largest generation," *Pew Research Center*, April 28, 2020, https://www.pewresearch.org/short-reads/2020/04/28/millennials-overtake-baby-boomers-as-americas-largest-generation/.

3.   Barbara A. Friedberg, "Are We in a Baby Boomer Retirement Crisis?" Investopedia, February 13, 2022, https://www.investopedia.com/articles/personal-finance/032216/are-we-baby-boomer-retirement-crisis.asp.

4.   David Burkus, "Why Amazon Bought Into Zappos's 'Pay to Quit' Policy," Inc.com, June 15, 2016, https://www.inc.com/david-burkus/why-amazon-bought-into-zappos-pay-to-quit-policy.html.

5.   Scott Krisiloff, "How Many Companies are There in the US?," Avondale Asset Management, May 23, 2012, http://avondaleassetmanagement.blogspot.com/2012/05/number-of-companies-in-us.html.

Chapter 4

1.   Author's note: I find the individual recruiters who can produce the longest, most specific list of details are also usually the worse recruiters. Why? Recruiters who are busting it calling a ton of candidates, screening like crazy, hiring nonstop, don't usually have time to remember all these little things they do! They're working, not trying to justify their job by remembering every single task they do. Your best recruiters will have a hard time listing all these details because this isn't where their attention is in their normal work, they're trying to close positions.

2.   Max Bitel, "High-Impact Visual Storytelling for Recruitment: Bringing HR Data To Life, Part 1," Visier, https://www.visier.com/blog/visual-storytelling-for-recruitment-part-1/.

3.   Tim Sackett, "The Single Point of Failure in Your Candidate Experience," The Talent Board, February 17, 2017, https://www. thetalentboard.org/article/single-point-failure-candidate-experience-thecandes/#.

4.   Updated Talent Board 2022 Candidate Experience report, https:// www.thetalentboard.org/press-releases/talent-board-releases-2022-candidate-experience-benchmark-research-report/.

Chapter 5

1.   Hillary Clinton, *It Takes a Village, Tenth Anniversary Edition* (New York: Simon and Schuster, 2006).

2.   Mel Robbins, *The 5 Second Rule: Transform Your Life, Work, and Confidence with Everyday Courage* (Nashville: Savio Republic, 2017).

3.   Lindsay Browning and Jean Martin, "Reinventing Recruiting in the New Work Environment," PowerPoint at CEB Corporate Leadership Council, June 11, 2015.

4.   Nellie Peshkov, "Building a Culture of Recruiting," filmed October 5, 2016 at LinkedInTalent Connect, Las Vegas, NV, video, 17:30, https://www.youtube.com/watch?v=ULxZY0otQaw.

Chapter 6

1.   Carmen Di Rito, "The Art of Unleashing Talent," *Stanford Social Innovation Review*, July 7, 2017, https://doi.org/10.48558/ 11QT-KZ49.

2.   Amazon, "2016 Letter to Shareholders," April 17, 2017, https:// www.aboutamazon.com/news/company-news/2016-letter-to-shareholders.

3. Sackett, Tim, "7 Things You Must Do if You Want to Hire the Best Team." The Tim Sackett Project, July 12, 2017, http://timsackett.com/2017/07/12/7-things-you-must-do-if-you-want-to-hire-the-best-team/.

4. Roger Connors and Tom Smith, *Journey to The Emerald City: Achieve a Competitive Edge by Creating a Culture of Accountability* (Hoboken: Prentice Hall Press, 2002).

Chapter 9

1. Personal interview.

2. Jessica Stillman, "Google's HR Boss: Focus on These Interview Questions," Inc.com, April 24, 2015, https://www.inc.com/jessica-stillman/google-s-hr-boss-use-these-interview-questions.html.

3. https://www.shrm.org/resourcesandtools/tools-and-samples/toolkits/pages/conductingbackgroundinvestigations.aspx.

Chapter 10

1. https://resources.symphonytalent.com/blog.

2. Shaunda Zilich GE likes to ask these questions.

3. Shaunda Zilich, in personal interview with author, October 2017.

4. https://www.slideshare.net/HROpenSource/be-a-digital-industrial-brand-ambassador-ge. https://youtu.be/N2-YrA9-FME?si=GeFLYHTMHpaxLYyB.

5. Linda Naiman, "Design Thinking as a Strategy for Innovation," Creativity at Work, October 27, 2023, https://www.creativityatwork.com/design-thinking-strategy-for-innovation/.

6.   Tim Brown, "Design Thinking," *Harvard Business Review*, June 2008, https://hbr.org/2008/06/design-thinking.

7.   Kendra Reay, "How Recruiting and HR Will Change in 2017, According to LinkedIn's Talent Leaders," LinkedIn Talent Blog, January 19, 2017, https://www.linkedin.com/business/talent/blog/talent-strategy/how-recruiting-and-hr-will-change.

8.   Haiyan Zhang and Sheri Feinzig, "Should I stay or should I go?" *Thought Leadership Whitepaper*, 2017, https://www.ibm.com/downloads/cas/08GZQKL1.

Chapter 11

1.   Satoshi Kanazawa, "Intelligence and Physical Attractiveness," *Intelligence* 39, no. 1 (February 2011): 7-14, https://doi.org/10.1016/j.intell.2010.11.003.

2.   David Engber, "Why Are Smart People Usually Ugly?" Slate, January 10, 2012, https://slate.com/technology/2012/01/are-smart-people-ugly-the-explainer-s-2011-question-of-the-year.html.

3.   Christopher A. Sanders, Alexis T. Jenkins, and Laura A. King, "Pretty, meaningful lives: physical attractiveness and experienced and perceived meaning in life," *The Journal of Positive Psychology* 18, no. 6 (2023): 978-994, https://www.tandfonline.com/doi/full/10.1080/17439760.2022.2155222.

Chapter 12

1.   Saba is a former HR tech company that was acquired by Cornerstone. https://www.youtube.com/watch?v=7ps8RKumhl4.

2.   Rob McIntosh personal interview with author.

3.   Greg Savage, "Re-Inventing KPIS for the Modern Recruiter," The Savage Recruitment Academy, June 28, 2016, https://www. gregsavage.com.au/2016/06/28/recruiter-kpis-from-crap-to-credible/.

Chapter 14

1.   Jessica Miller-Merrell, "The Why Behind HR Technology's Hype Cycle," Workology, May 20, 2014, https://workology.com/ hr-technology-adoption-cycle.

2.   Jim Collins, *Good to Great: Why Some Companies Make the Leap and Others Don't* (New York: Harper Business Publishing, 2001).

3.   https://rfpodcast.com/.

4.   https://www.bls.gov/tus/latest-numbers.htm.

5.   Hannah Morgan, "7 Things You Should Know About Employee Referrals," U.S. News and World Report, October 7, 2015, https://money.usnews.com/money/blogs/outside-voices-careers/2015/10/07/7-things-you-should-know-about-employee-referrals.

Bibliography

Chapter 1

Bock, Laszlo. *Work Rules!: Insights from Inside Google That Will Transform How You Live and Lead.* New York: Twelve, 2015.

Perrin, Andrew and Sara Atske. "7% of Americans don't use the internet. Who are they?" *Pew Research Center*, April 2, 2021. https://www.pewresearch.org/short-reads/2021/04/02/7-of-americans-dont-use-the-internet-who-are-they/.

Chapter 2

Burkus, David. "Why Amazon Bought Into Zappos's 'Pay to Quit' Policy." *Inc.com*, June 15, 2016. https://www.inc.com/david-burkus/why-amazon-bought-into-zappos-pay-to-quit-policy.html.

Centers for Disease Control and Prevention. "Productive Aging and Work." Last modified March 15, 2023. https://www.cdc.gov/niosh/topics/productiveaging/default.html.

Friedberg, Barbara A. "Are We in a Baby Boomer Retirement Crisis?" Investopedia. February 13, 2022. https://www.investopedia.com/articles/personal-finance/032216/are-we-baby-boomer-retirement-crisis.asp.

Fry, Richard. "Millennials overtake Baby Boomers as America's largest generation." *Pew Research Center*, April 28, 2020. https://www.pewresearch.org/short-reads/2020/04/28/millennials-overtake-baby-boomers-as-americas-largest-generation/.

Krisiloff, Scott. "Employment and Competitiveness of Small Businesses." Avondale Asset Management. November 15, 2012. http://avondaleassetmanagement.blogspot.com/2012/11/employment-and-competitiveness-of-small.html.

Chapter 4

Bitel, Max. "High-Impact Visual Storytelling for Recruitment: Bringing HR Data To Life, Part 1." Visier. https://www.visier.com/blog/visual-storytelling-for-recruitment-part-1/.
Sackett, Tim. "The Single Point of Failure in Your Candidate Experience." The Talent Board, February 17, 2017. https://www.thetalentboard.org/article/single-point-failure-candidate-experience-thecandes/#.

Chapter 5

Browning, Lindsay and Jean Martin. "Reinventing Recruiting in the New Work Environment." PowerPoint at CEB Corporate Leadership Council, June 11, 2015.
Clinton, Hillary. *It Takes a Village, Tenth Anniversary Edition*. New York: Simon & Schuster, 2006.
Peshkov, Nellie. "Building a Culture of Recruiting." Filmed October 2016 at LinkedInTalent Connect, Las Vegas, NV. Video.
Robbins, Mel. *The 5 Second Rule: Transform Your Life, Work, and Confidence with Everyday Courage*. Savio Republic, 2017.

Chapter 6

Amazon. "2016 Letter to Shareholders." April 17, 2017. https://www.aboutamazon.com/news/company-news/2016-letter-to-shareholders.
Connors, Roger and Tom Smith. *Journey to The Emerald City: Achieve a Competitive Edge by Creating a Culture of Accountability*. Hoboken: Prentice Hall Press, 2002.

Di Rito, Carmen. "The Art of Unleashing Talent." *Stanford Social Innovation Review*, 2017. https://doi.org/10.48558/11QT-KZ49.

Sackett, Tim. "7 Things You Must Do if You Want to Hire the Best Team." The Tim Sackett Project. July 12, 2017. http://timsackett.com/2017/07/12/7-things-you-must-do-if-you-want-to-hire-the-best-team/.

Chapter 9

Society for Human Resources Management. "Conducting Background Investigations and Reference Checks." https://www.shrm.org/resourcesandtools/tools-and-samples/toolkits/pages/conductingbackgroundinvestigations.aspx.

Stillman, Jessica. "Google's HR Boss: Focus on These Interview Questions," *Inc.com*, April 24, 2015. https://www.inc.com/jessica-stillman/google-s-hr-boss-use-these-interview-questions.html.

Chapter 10

Brown, Tim. "Design Thinking." *Harvard Business Review*, June 2008. https://hbr.org/2008/06/design-thinking.

Naiman, Linda. "Design Thinking as a Strategy for Innovation." Creativity at Work. October 27, 2023. https://www.creativityatwork.com/design-thinking-strategy-for-innovation/.

Reay, Kendra. "How Recruiting and HR Will Change in 2017, According to LinkedIn's Talent Leaders." LinkedIn Talent Blog. January 19, 2017. https://www.linkedin.com/business/talent/blog/talent-strategy/how-recruiting-and-hr-will-change.

Zhang, Haiyan and Sheri Feinzig. "Should I stay or should I go?" *Thought Leadership Whitepaper*, 2017. https://www.ibm.com/downloads/cas/08GZQKL1.

Zilich, Shaunda, in personal interview with author, October 2017.

Rally. "What is Recruitment Marketing?" https://rallyrecruitmentmarketing.com/what-is-recruitment-marketing/.

Chapter 11

Engber, David. "Why Are Smart People Usually Ugly?" Slate. January 10, 2012. https://slate.com/technology/2012/01/are-smart-people-ugly-the-explainer-s-2011-question-of-the-year.html.

Kanazawa, Satoshi. "Intelligence and Physical Attractiveness." *Intelligence* 39, no. 1 (February 2011): 7-14. https://doi.org/10.1016/j.intell.2010.11.003.

Sanders, Christopher A., Alexis T. Jenkins, and Laura A. King, "Pretty, meaningful lives: physical attractiveness and experienced and perceived meaning in life." *The Journal of Positive Psychology* 18, no. 6 (2023): 978-994. https://www.tandfonline.com/doi/full/10.1080/17439760.2022.2155222.

Chapter 12

Savage, Greg. "Re-Inventing KPIS for the Modern Recruiter." The Savage Recruitment Academy. June 28, 2016. https://www.gregsavage.com.au/2016/06/28/recruiter-kpis-from-crap-to-credible/.

Chapter 14

Collins, Jim. *From Good to Great: Why Some Companies Make the Leap and Others Don't.* New York: HarperBusiness, 2001. Retrieved from https://www.amazon.com/Good-Great-Some-Companies-Others/dp/0066620996/ref=tmm_hrd_swatch_0?_encoding=UTF8&qid=&sr=.

Index

About SHRM Books

SHRM Books develops and publishes insights, ideas, strategies, and solutions on the topics that matter most to human resource professionals, people managers, and students.

The strength of our program lies in the expertise and thought leadership of our authors to educate, empower, elevate, and inspire readers around the world.

Each year SHRM Books publishes new titles covering contemporary human resource management issues, as well as general workplace topics. With more than one hundred titles available in print, digital, and audio formats, SHRM's books can be purchased through SHRMStore.org and a variety of book retailers.

Learn more at shrm.org/books.